STAR+GATE

STAR+GATE

KEYS TO THE KINGDOM

BY

RICHARD H. GEER

EDITED BY

DONALD KOUE

VINTAGE BOOKS
A DIVISION OF RANDOM HOUSE
N E W   Y O R K

ACKNOWLEDGMENTS

Although I may have the fortune of having my name placed on this book and on the other parts of STAR+GATE, there were many people who assisted in its development and progress. The joy of discovery and the pains of birthing STAR+GATE were primarily mine, yet this has always been a project that attracted the interest and talents of many. So many were involved, in fact, that it would be impossible here to list and thank them all. Each of you know who you are, and whether your contribution was major or small, I thank you for what you did. Each of you gave selflessly, and together our efforts made STAR+GATE a reality. You have my sincere gratitude.

R.H.G.

CONTENTS

● ▲ ✦ ▼ ✕ ▪ ■

INTRODUCTION

WHAT IS STAR+GATE? WHY DO YOU USE IT?

STAR+GATE can be called a game, a tool, a system, a process, or an experience, and each of these terms is accurate. STAR+GATE is all of these, yet no single word can truly express what it is. Why? Because STAR+GATE is about you, the individual, and the way you operate. It's about what you *think*, what you *feel*, and it exists to show you the power of *how you see*.

Briefly, using STAR+GATE entails thinking of a topic to explore, shuffling and drawing special cards, placing them in positions on a "spread" layout that shows aspects of a situation, then developing a specific interpretation for the cards through a step-by-step process aimed at achieving clarity about real issues.

STAR+GATE is an adventure into your own experience of life. With it you can clarify and understand situations more clearly. You can identify your own motivations and goals. And you can discover your own valid methods for improving or enhancing circumstances.

In a world of increasing complexity and busy-ness, STAR + GATE can be used as a method for taking the time out to see and understand why things are the way they are for you.

"Whatever happened to my *creativity?*" "Why didn't I use my *imagination?*" "How am I going to get out of this *mess?*" When relevant questions such as these arise, they deserve attention—as do many others we ask ourselves.

The STAR + GATE system was conceived to help people address those parts of life where more needs to be known than is already known—that is, to expand one's conscious awareness. When you can see a situation for what it truly is, you will also be able to see how it is being viewed or approached. It is then that the real key to change is at hand; it is then that increased conscious awareness is coupled with an understanding of the individual's role in shaping circumstances.

STAR + GATE is a unique environment in which to gain awareness and insight. It provides a language of symbols, the living alphabet of the mind. Such a language permits access to awareness of what the mind knows, both consciously and subconsciously. Not only will using STAR + GATE seem to mirror actual situations, revealing factors that may have been hidden from view, but it will also allow conscious recognition, thereby opening many other levels of the psyche.

HOW DOES IT WORK?

STAR + GATE helps you tap—and develop—your intuitive insight.

This kind of activity has also been called divination, from *divine*—pertaining to God or godlike. In the past, divining seemed to be the exclusive property of seers or prophets, people who might be perceived as anything from a messenger of God to a clever fake. The tools modern society has inherited for achieving insight—such as the I Ching, Tarot, the Runes, and others—carry with them their own mystique and, in some cases, superstition. Mystery seems to have prevailed around the idea of seeing past the moment or beyond appearances.

Yet there is enough known today about the inherent capabilities of man to enable each person to rightly claim his or her own gift for insight as a basic ingredient for living—without unnecessary mystique.

How do you tap this intuitive insight? Where do you go when you really need answers? Just about anywhere. But many people, whether they are looking inside themselves or turning outside for help, find only confusion.

STAR+GATE is a tool for clearing away the confusion. It is based in part on the idea that there is no real dividing line between the inside and the outside, between the self and not-self, the dreamer and the dream, between you and others. STAR+GATE is a carefully conceived mirroring device based on the principles of life itself. When you look into the mirror created by STAR+GATE, you see a symbolic portrait of yourself. This portrait may please you or challenge you or upset you. You may reject it or allow it to inspire you. But the picture is always your own.

One of the active concepts in STAR+GATE is *synchronicity,* a term first used by Jung. It suggests that the link between apparently unrelated events in your life is you, your understanding and insight—your point of view. Only you can give special meaning to these events. What happens to you in life, then, belongs expressly to you. No one will ever have quite the same perspective on the world or experience things the way you do. Everything that happens to you is in synchronization with your particular life. It is all a reflection of you.

Using STAR+GATE, its symbols and framework, is also uniquely in step with the rest of your life. What you see and comprehend through STAR+GATE will indeed be a reflection of yourself. And you will see that the reflection is one in which you participate, one that will vividly depict your reality, that will contain the "answers" or personal tools for improving situations.

With STAR+GATE, you make the choices. You decide what question to ask, what subject to explore, what the cards and other aspects mean. You decide how to utilize the symbols and how best to approach your life. The opportunity to respond so freely to a tool may seem unusual at first, but it was created to help you become more aware of the choices you make. STAR+GATE is also based on the belief that one's truth is never out of reach, and that attaining it does not have to be difficult.

WHEN TO USE STAR + GATE

Use it when you need it.

For most people, today's world is a busy and demanding one. Time can be a precious commodity, especially time for seeing things in perspective and with clarity. Once familiar with the tool, using STAR + GATE on a regular basis will take only a few moments and can easily be made a part of your personal routine. It can be used on a daily, weekly, or other basis to monitor progress on a specific situation. Or it can be used as situations occur.

Just as the physical body benefits from exercise, so does the mind. Allow yourself the time, as part of your own way of doing things, to look into yourself and understand your viewpoint on the happenings in your life. This is a method for adding to the most meaningful knowledge there is, your own. So give yourself the time to know yourself better.

THE PARTS OF STAR + GATE

STAR + GATE has two main parts: the ninety-six Symbolic Cards and the Circle Pattern. This book will explain and acquaint you with both components and give you the basis for using each to explore personal topics.

The cards (as a set) and the Circle Pattern are each ways of viewing the whole individual. The Circle Pattern can be thought of as a map, and the cards as pieces of the map. In that respect, each part equals the other, and each equals "you" with your many facets.

The cards show the "sides" of a person through the medium of common symbols (including related keywords and groupings of symbols). The Circle Pattern shows these aspects collected into a complete design—the total person—so that relative positions of symbols and connections among them can be seen. Numbers and letter designations on the cards correspond to locations on the circle.

The cards are the experiential part of STAR + GATE; the Circle Pattern the framework of the tool, the organization behind the cards. The STAR+GATE Circle Pattern is oriented to the *context* of the individual; the cards or symbols to the *content*.

Since the Symbolic Cards are visually engaging and evoke mental associations, they are the part of STAR+GATE most people become familiar with first. There are a variety of ways these cards can be used, including the Sky Spread (showing present, past, and future aspects of a situation), the Goal Spread (aimed at achieving a desired result), a spread for relationships, and uses for children. All of these are explained in the book.

Typically, the Circle Pattern is used as an adjunct to the cards after they have been generated and interpreted using one of the spreads. Plotting symbols within the circle, viewing their positions, connections, and other visible relationships can yield additional perspective on the topic being explored. Such "mapping" on the circle can also indicate trends of the individual within a classic twelvefold Cycle of Growth.

These parts of STAR+GATE are your "Keys to the Kingdom," the tools to use to tap the knowing within each individual. What follows in this book will show you how to use each part to help you in your own discovery.

USING
STAR+GATE

● ▲ ✦ ▼ ✕ ◼ ■

THE TURNING-ABOUT

The turning-about is upon us,
the turning of mind, the expansion of eyes,
the presence of children who bathe
in the light of the stars;
their distant brothers move closer,
cherish the light that shapes from within.

Our heritage,
the spirit who soars,
the mind that dreams,
the heart that reaches out.

O, children of creation, the island of light
is within you.
As you reach for your home in the Sun,
the lamp of your becoming
strikes brilliance everywhere—
you are free.

Richard H. Geer

USING **STAR+GATE**

I n this section, you will be introduced to the STAR+GATE cards and learn the various ways to use them on the Sky Spread to gain insight into topics of interest to you. For some people, the techniques of the Sky Spread are enough, but there is a deeper level of understanding available through STAR+GATE's Circle Pattern. An explanation of the Circle Pattern, which visually shows the relationship among the symbols, begins on page 163.

If STAR+GATE is new to you, take a few minutes to look through the cards. There is a great variety of symbols in the cards, but most of them are common to everyday experiences. Each also has a name and a series of keywords, all designed to help you evoke mental associations.

A brief explanation of the cards (there is a lengthier one in "The Ninety-six Symbolic Cards," page 43) is followed by instructions on how to use the Sky Spread. Also included is an example of how one person utilized the Sky Spread; this will help you to realize the potential in your own use of the spread. Suggestions for other ways in which to use STAR+GATE concludes this section. This includes how to use STAR+GATE with others and more details on the Sky Spread framework.

THE SYMBOLIC CARDS

There are ninety-six STAR+GATE cards—**A** through **L** and **1** through **84**—and they are two-sided, with a picture side and a word side. Each card has a name, a number, a picture, a Card Type symbol, and a series of keywords. Each element expresses a facet of the overall symbol. The number shows where the symbol fits into the Circle Pattern (you won't use it in the Sky Spread). The name of the card summons mental associations, both rational and intuitive, because a name can remind one of everyday things and also connect with deep-seated subconscious realities. The picture on the card is also intended to stimulate both conscious and subconscious associations—connections that are seldom rational in nature yet are real in their own right. The keywords, on the other hand, stimulate the more rational and structured search for meaning. There is a formula or style to the word series for each type of card; this will become apparent with use.

The Card Type symbol denotes the group of cards to which the symbol belongs. It expresses the level of approach of the card, a factor that adds to the overall meaning.

All the elements, through their own form, point to what the card *can* mean to the user. But it is through the process of interpretation that the player develops his or her own specific meaning, based on personal viewpoint and the situation being explored. No card has any strict meaning, and any card can have multiple meanings, all valid, for a particular player. It all depends on how the player sees the symbols in terms of himself or herself, and this can vary greatly over time and circumstances.

An analysis of each card, in alphabetical and numerical order, can be found in "The Ninety-six Symbolic Cards" (see page 43). These descriptions can help you find the meaning of each card that is appropriate for you in a given situation.

THE SKY SPREAD LAYOUT

The Sky Spread layout enables you to display the STAR+GATE cards in a way that makes a symbolic statement about a personal topic. Three cards represent factors in the past or the background of a situation—in areas labeled "Behind You" and "New Focus." Three other cards show events that are still forming—labeled "Ahead of You" and "New Focus." Four cards describe the present moment from which the individual's choices are being made— "You Now," "The Issue," "Helping," and "Distracting."

Everything you see in a particular spread arrangement will relate specifically to the topic you select. Therefore it is important to be clear about what it is you want to know.

The subject you choose to explore can be anything that matters to you, anything that you want insights about. It can be a serious topic or one chosen more for the fun of it. It can be about an everyday matter or about a long-term situation. The topic can be highly specific or rather general in nature. It is suggested that the topic *not* be expressed as a question. The woman who wants to know "Should I marry Tom?" will get clearer insights into the matter if she chooses something like "Marrying Tom" as her topic. In this way, she will receive a symbolic picture about getting married and hopefully make up her mind from what she discovers, rather than expecting the cards to tell her yes or no. In fact, in this example, the primary concern might be the woman's desire to stay single. Therefore, her topic might better be stated as "Staying Single."

Choose your topic as clearly and simply as you can. Try to express it in just a few words, possibly writing it down so you can refer to it.

Keeping your topic in mind, mix or shuffle the entire set of cards. Do this in any way that is most comfortable to you. It is suggested that the cards' picture side be face down or away from you, to minimize any conscious recognition of cards while shuffling. When the cards are thoroughly mixed, put them in a neat stack in front of you, keeping the picture side down. Cut the deck, putting the bottom pile on the top of the deck. (With a new set of cards, be especially thorough in shuffling. The cards in a new deck are grouped in numerical order, which means that each Card Type is grouped, the way a new set of playing cards has all four suits in order.)

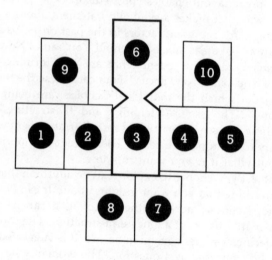

Draw the top card off the deck and place it *picture side up* in the box numbered "1" on the Sky Spread. Draw the next card off the top and place it, again *picture side up,* in the box numbered "2" on the spread. Continue, drawing the next card off the deck, placing it in the box numbered "3" and so on until each of the ten boxes is filled with a single card. Any reversed cards should be turned to face you, and all ten cards should be picture side up.

The recommended way of using STAR+GATE, as just explained, is to deal cards from the deck after it has been shuffled to your satisfaction. However, some people are not comfortable with this method. If you prefer, you may choose the cards you want to fill the positions in the Sky Spread (or any other layout). When cards are selected in this manner, make your choice based on the picture side of the cards. This will allow you to continue through the full process of interpretation as described below.

INTERPRETING CARDS IN THE SKY SPREAD—THE SIX-STEP PROCESS

You are now ready to interpret the cards. The interpretation uses a six-step method. A brief summary is presented first for quick reference; this is followed by the detailed interpretation.

To fully develop the value of the cards you received, carefully follow the steps. Once you are familiar with STAR+GATE, the process of interpreting the cards will be easier and take less time.

Each step of the process is different and involves using your mind in different ways. Some parts may seem unusual or confusing at first. But try the process as it is presented; each step can unlock valuable answers. And remember: You have the ultimate choice in deciding what the cards mean and how to integrate these insights into your life.

SUMMARY OF THE SIX-STEP PROCESS

DEVELOPING YOUR MEANING

1. **Instant impressions:** On picture side of cards, give your initial meanings to symbols based on visual impressions.

2. **Discover words and card types:** Turn to word side of cards; consider types of cards received and the series of keywords.

3. **Determine card meanings:** Decide what each card means to you in terms of topic, turning each back to picture side, and letting the picture serve as a reminder of meaning chosen.

TAPPING INNER MEANINGS

4. **Envisioning:** Using the groups of symbols, imagine a simple scene or a quick story. The interaction of the symbols most easily imagined will reveal intuitive awareness about topic. Meanings given to individual symbols now combine into areas of meaning and awareness.

   Envision picture stories with these groups of cards:

   past — cards labeled "Behind You" with "Old Focus"
   future — cards "Ahead of You" with "New Focus"
   present — the "Helping" with the "Distracting" cards,
           then "You Now" with "The Issue."

   (As you complete each story, remove that group of cards from the spread until only the last pair is left.)

CREATE A PLAN OF ACTION

5. **Transform "Now":** Consciously imagine the Best Picture, the most positive interaction of the "You Now" with "The Issue" symbols. This represents a change (or improvement) in outlook on the topic. Decide what course of action or revised approach your picture represents.

6. **Level of Approach:** As the STAR+GATE process is completed, determine current "Level of Approach" (based on Card Types) as a benchmark for change and progress with topic.

DEVELOPING YOUR MEANING

STEP 1.
Instant Impressions

With the picture side of the cards facing you, look through the Sky Spread and think about how each card relates to your topic. Don't try to resolve your topic at this time. Instead, freely associate with the symbols and gather impressions of the way the visual images relate to the subject you chose.

Below is an explanation of the Sky Spread terms.

PRESENT The center area of the Sky Spread represents the here and now. Four symbols make up this core from which the other symbols (and information) in the spread are viewed.

The box labeled *The Issue* on the Sky Spread represents what is at issue about your topic, symbolically an underlying reason, purpose, or focus of attention. *You Now* symbolizes where you are right now, in terms of "The Issue" and in terms of your topic. The *Helping* symbol indicates something aiding you in dealing with "The Issue" and the topic. Next to it is the *Distracting* card, which stands for something that is diverting your attention away from resolving the topic. These are the four cards that have the most immediate bearing on the topic.

PAST To the left of the central cards are three that deal with the past and show how present conditions came to be. There are two labeled *Behind You,* which suggest significant experiences that have led to "You Now." Above them is the *Old Focus,* indicating an earlier issue or purpose related to your topic, one that prevailed before now and has in some way led to the present focus ("The Issue").

FUTURE To the right of the central cards are three that deal with the future, two are labeled *Ahead of You,* the third, above them, is *New Focus.* These indicate where things are headed based on where things are right now. Any future is flexible and depends on how matters are dealt with in the present—in other words, the way you see the "You Now" symbol interacting with "The Issue." If you like what you see in the symbols in the future area, you may want to continue the way "You Now" is interacting with "The Issue" in the spread.

STEP 2.
Discover Words and Card Types

Next, turn the cards over to the word side. Read the series of keywords related to each symbol and consider how the ideas expressed relate to a card's position in the spread and to your topic. You may also want to read about the symbols in the "Card Information" section of this book (see page 25).

In addition, take into account the types of cards received in your spread. Card Types are shown on the cards' word side in colored symbols. There are seven types in all, and they represent the different Levels of Approach involved in personal situations. The significance of Card Types is shown in the chart below, they are briefly stated on the Sky Spread itself and are explained in more detail at the beginning of the "Card Information" section.

The Card Types (also called Levels of Approach) are a major feature of STAR+GATE, being derived from the system's Circle Pattern, which maps and groups aspects of the self. The seven types show a spectrum of personal experience ranging from inner ways of feeling satisfaction to outer energetic qualities.

Look at the placement and distribution of the Card Types in your Sky Spread. What patterns do you see? Do you notice any symmetries, clusters, or repetitions? As your experience with STAR+GATE grows, the Card Types and their positions in a spread become more meaningful. You can also see that keywords for the cards are presented differently for each Card Type.

THE SEVEN CARD TYPES

In reviewing Card Types in the spread, consider the meanings of each type. For example, a Sign card representing fulfillment might appear in the "You Now" position in the spread. This can be thought of as the player identifying with one kind of fulfillment but perhaps preparing for a new means of satisfaction. Or a Key (challenge) card may appear in the "Helping" position, indicating a certain challenge is actually helping to resolve a situation. Each array of cards is unique and provides an opportunity to explore placement of the Card Types.

This step may take a few minutes, but the time taken to consider the information each card contains and the thoughts that are stimulated as a result is time well spent.

THE SEVEN CARD TYPES

STARS ● —ENERGIES, moods, atmospheres that surround you.

STATES ▲ —CONDITIONS, environments, states of things.

STAR-CROSSES ✦ —SELF-EXPRESSIONS, ways of acting, ways of being perceived by others.

GIFTS ▼ —TALENTS, abilities, skills.

KEYS ✕ —CHALLENGES, REALIZATIONS, confrontations about living.

GATES ▮ —ATTITUDES, approaches, ways of dealing with situations.

SIGNS ■ —FULFILLMENT, ways of feeling satisfaction.

STEP 3.
Decide on Meaning

After you note your first impressions of the cards' pictures and review keywords and Card Types, it is time to come to some conclusions about what each card means for you.

Start with any one card whose meaning you feel you understand. As best you can, decide how that card applies to your topic. Turn it back to the picture side and let the visual symbol serve as a reminder of the meaning you chose. Go on to another card. Reach your conclusions about its meaning. Turn the card back to the picture side, again letting the picture be a reminder of the meaning you have decided on. Continue through the other cards in the spread, in whatever order you want. When this step is finished, all the cards should be picture side up.

TAPPING INNER MEANINGS

STEP 4.
Envisioning

The mind holds more information about your situation than you realize. A creative visualizing technique called Picture Stories will lead you to your inner awareness. This is one of the most valuable parts of the STAR+GATE process, although it may seem difficult at first. You will be looking at groups of cards in the spread and envisioning scenes with them; these scenes will tell a revealing story about your topic.

THE PAST First, look at the three cards in the area of the past, the two "Behind You" and the "Old Focus." Let yourself imagine a single scene made up of these three symbols. Do not be concerned about what the picture looks like; just freely imagine *one* scene that contains the elements from these three cards.

For example, if the three cards are the Chest, the Tree, and the Rain, the picture imagined might be that of a chest buried in the ground next to a tree, with rain coming down eroding the ground and uncovering the top of the chest. Or the picture might be one in which you see yourself carrying the chest and taking shelter from the rain under the tree. You can always put yourself in the scene as a catalyst to bring the various symbols together. This is especially useful when the symbols are inanimate; it is revealing in a special way.

Once you have imagined a scene with your cards in the past, the next step is to find out what it means. The picture you have created is a very simple story of how you see the symbols interacting. Now recall the meanings you gave to the individual symbols and see those meanings interacting in the same way. This is a story about how you see the past of the situation. The story suggests how the present circumstances came about. No matter how fanciful the story, it may provide *sudden recognitions,* flashes of insight that bear on the topic and make it more easily understood. When you have finished doing this, remove these three cards from the spread.

THE FUTURE Follow the same process with the three cards in the future—the two "Ahead of You" and the "New Focus." Imagine a single scene composed of these three symbols, then take a mental step back and look at the interactions of the symbols. Recall the meanings given to the symbols and see how these interact. Discover the story about how you see the future that is contained in this picture. Again, when you are finished, remove these cards from the spread.

HELPING AND DISTRACTING Now form a picture story with the "Helping" and "Distracting" cards. How do they interact in one scene? What meanings have you given these cards, and how do they interact? This is a story about the pluses and minuses involved in the situation. When you are finished, remove these cards from the spread.

YOU AND THE ISSUE You now have two cards left on the spread—"You Now" and "The Issue." Form a scene using just these two cards (and yourself if desired). Be open and honest in imagining what this picture looks like. See how the elements interact, then recall the meanings of the cards and see how they interact. This is a very important picture; it shows how you see yourself with the issues at hand in terms of your topic.

CREATING A PLAN OF ACTION

STEP 5.
Transforming "Now"

Making a positive plan of action is the next step. No matter what story you formed with the "You Now" and "Issue" cards, it can be improved. Work with these two cards again, but instead of just imagining any picture, deliberately form a scene that is the most *positive* and *constructive* one possible. Be kind to yourself. Any situation has a number of possible outcomes. Choose the best possible outcome, using the elements of the symbols themselves. If in the previous story (Step 4) you seemed to "lose," can you now see a way to use the symbols differently so that you "win"?

Make your Best Picture. See how "You Now" and "The Issue" interact in the most desirable way. Then use the meaning given to each card to determine a course of action for improving or resolving the situation in real life. Based on your picture, consider new approaches and ways of acting that will carry this symbolic plan into action.

STEP 6.
Level of Approach

The cards have now been interpreted, and your process with the Sky Spread is nearly complete. As a final step, it is helpful to know your current Level of Approach, so you can use it as a benchmark for change and progress in your topic when you use STAR+GATE again.

To find your level, look at the word side of the "You Now" card. Find its Card Type, then look up its level in the list below.

Based on Card Types in the STAR+GATE system, no level is actually better or worse than another, yet each is distinct. In any given situation, you may want to be at a different level or to stay in the one you are in. In order to achieve improvement, it always helps to know what you can about where you are as well as what you want to attain.

Star — Level of Radiance—Participating in a pervading mood or atmosphere that affects those around you as well as yourself.

State — Level of Circumstance—Giving credit to outside conditions when things go well, blaming circumstances when there are difficulties.

Star-Cross — Level of Expression—Expressing yourself to the world, but with a concern for how others will see you.

Gift — Level of Qualities—Developing and demonstrating inner gifts, talents, and qualities.

15

Key — Level of Challenge—Facing present issues head on and realizing that the tools for change are at hand, though often disguised.

Gate — Level of Attitude—Recognizing limiting beliefs and developing and fine-tuning new attitudes.

Sign — Level of Fulfillment—Feeling satisfied and complete within, yet preparing to seek new kinds of satisfaction.

ANN'S SKY SPREAD

To help you understand the whole process, here is the experience of one person using STAR+GATE to help her gain insight into a personal concern. Her analysis of her STAR+GATE cards will be useful to you in learning how to analyze your own Symbolic Cards.

Ann is a young working mother with two children. Her topic, the behavior of her six-year-old daughter, is the sort many of us have in life—a situation in which our own actions may be crucial in improving a relationship. Her daughter's behavior was not extreme or abnormal, yet there were things Ann did not like, and she wondered about her own role in the child's development. She brought the problem to STAR+GATE. In line with earlier advice about posing the problem not as a question but as a simple statement, thus opening wide the doors of intuition instead of trying to squeeze them down to "yes" or "no" responses, Ann stated her topic as "My relationship with my daughter."

The cards she received are shown on the facing page.

STEP 1.
Instant Impressions

Ann quickly looked through her spread of cards and described her initial impressions about each card in relation to the topic. In the area of the past, she saw the Star of Impulse as a focus representing scattered energy. It was descriptive to her of the lack of direction in their relationship and that they had just been reacting to one

ANN'S SKY SPREAD

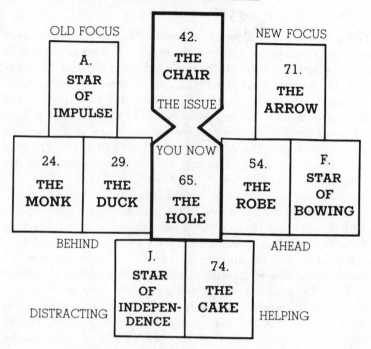

OLD FOCUS

A. STAR OF IMPULSE

42. THE CHAIR
THE ISSUE

NEW FOCUS

71. THE ARROW

24. THE MONK

29. THE DUCK

YOU NOW
65. THE HOLE

54. THE ROBE

F. STAR OF BOWING

BEHIND

J. STAR OF INDEPEN- DENCE

74. THE CAKE

AHEAD

DISTRACTING

HELPING

another. The symbol of the Monk reminded her of her daughter—uncommunicative. The Duck she saw as herself in the past, trying to make things work but floundering. All three of those symbols painted an accurate picture of how things had been.

In the area of the present, she saw the "You Now" card, the Hole, as very appropriate, the mother opening but directing things from her point of view. She saw the Chair as "The Issue" as their working together; it symbolized a place where they could both sit side by side. The "Helping" card, the Cake, she saw as a symbol of giving between mother and daughter. The "Distracting" card, the Star of Independence, was seen as personal pride that got in each other's way. "Ahead" of her, she saw the Robe as stability and calmness, and the Star of Bowing as getting along with each other, working together. Above those symbols was the "New Focus," the Arrow, which she perceived as a positive direction for their relationship.

17

STEP 2.
Discover Words and Card Types

The cards were then turned to the word side, and Ann considered both the Card Types and the words that were on each card. In doing so, she began to change her mind about some of her symbols. Discovering that the two cards "Behind" her were Starcrosses, she recognized that both the Monk and Duck represented divergent ways she had expressed herself in the relationship. One was very inward, the other more outward—the result seeming almost two-faced. This occurred under the "Old Focus" of a Star and indicated undirected energy that surrounded her and her daughter.

It was very appropriate to her that the "You Now" card was a Gate card, indicating attitudes and approaches, exactly her present concern, as well as the fact that Openness was involved. Learning that "The Issue" card was a Gift, Ann saw the Chair symbol as opportunity, that she and her daughter could work together but that it would take effort, give and take. Looking at the "Helping" card, the Cake, as a Sign or fulfillment aspect, Ann saw that give and take at the moment was more focused on rewards and physical satisfaction than on emotional gratification. Seeing a Star (of Independence) in the "Distracting" box, she viewed its energy as the desire to be apart rather than cooperate together.

Looking at the cards "Ahead" of her, Ann discovered that the Robe, which she had first seen as a kind of stability, was a Key or challenge card that had to do with roles. She recognized that each person's role in the relationship might well become challenging, but that it could indeed lead to realizations for both of them. The Star of Bowing (also "Ahead") with its energy of Integrating showed her that they really could create an atmosphere of cooperation. Ann saw the "New Focus" of the Arrow as her ability to point the relationship in the right direction through Decisiveness and Spontaneity.

STEP 3.
Decide on Meaning

In Ann's case, she had been developing conclusions about her cards in the first two steps, and she found it easy to express what each symbol meant. She went through the spread, highlighting each card's meaning, then turning it back to the picture side. The pictures reinforced the conclusions she had already made.

STEP 4.
Envisioning

Now Ann's spread became animated and revealing as she began to play with pictures in her mind. First, she looked at the three symbols in the past, the Star of Impulse, Monk, and Duck. She imagined a picture of a Monk with a Duck's face under the hood and the agitated light of impulsiveness shining around the figure. When asked what she thought the picture meant, Ann answered it was like constantly being at odds with herself, a sort of Jekyll and Hyde, not knowing how to act. To her, this truly portrayed her dilemma of the past.

Next, she imagined a picture with the cards in the area of the future, the Arrow, Robe, and Star of Bowing. She saw herself wearing a robe of stature, holding an arrow with the light of Integrating all around her. To Ann, this represented a personal sense of direction, of knowing how to act and making her approach fit the situation. This was the picture of how she wanted the relationship to turn out.

With the "Helping" and "Distracting" cards, she saw the Cake glowing in the light of Independence. Here, the positive and negative influences switched roles. She found the symbol of material rewards transformed by the Star of Independence into a symbol of rewards without motives. In her words, the Cake now symbolized "no guilt, no strokes, just sincerity."

With her "You Now" and "Issue" cards, she saw the Chair sitting on the grass next to the Hole. To Ann, this meant an outer aspect of herself (the Chair) being in a better position to utilize her more open, inner perspective (the Hole). She liked seeing these symbols side by side, each aspect helping the other. Yet, in a way, they did not interact with each other. They just sat there, beside each other.

STEP 5.
Transform "Now"

Here Ann had the opportunity to create the best-looking picture possible, and to see what it might indicate in terms of a new approach.

In her mind, she played with the same two symbols for a few minutes, and then she announced that she had put them together. She had placed the Hole *on* the Chair, integrating the inner and outer aspects of herself. She interpreted this to mean that she could trust her inner feelings about how she should act, that she had sensed how to respond to situations with her daughter in the past but had avoided putting it all together.

She had to laugh at the fact that the picture now looked like a child's potty chair. Yet that turned out to be meaningful. Ann, as a mother, knew better than anyone else each step in her daughter's development. She knew when her child had outgrown diapers and could begin using a potty chair. And when the potty chair was mastered, the mother removed it. The symbol indicated the mother's ability to know what is best for the child and to use whatever tools are appropriate to help the child grow up. It became Ann's reminder of her role as a mother in raising the child.

STEP 6.
Level of Approach

Ann briefly took note of the Card Type of her "You Now" card. As a Gate, it indicated dealing with the situation from the Level of Attitude. The emphasis was quite aptly on dealing with her own attitudes about relating to her daughter.

MORE ABOUT THE SKY SPREAD

The following is provided for those who would like more information on aspects of the Sky Spread and about interpreting symbols within its framework.

1. **NAME OF THE SPREAD** Early man gazed into the expanse of the night sky, most likely pondering his purpose on Earth

and the nature of the universe that surrounded him. At a time that preceded recorded history, man projected his thoughts and dreams into patterns of stars in the heavens. There were his gods, his warriors and other mythic archetypes, in a library of starry patterns that returned to his view night after night. The name of the basic STAR+GATE layout was chosen as the Sky Spread to tap back into that prehistoric heritage so that one might imagine the Symbolic Cards appearing out of the wonder of the night sky.

2. THE SPREAD'S STORY LINE   The numbered boxes one through five on the spread represent a story about the player in terms of his or her topic. There are two boxes about the past ("Behind You"), one about the present ("You Now"), and two about the future ("Ahead of You"). The cards received in these places represent the person himself, regardless of the types of cards involved. It can be helpful to look at the story line of the spread, and to see how one symbol begins the story (#1), which leads to the next (#2), and so on, with the story ending at the box on the far right (#5). The key to the story line is always in the center, the present "You Now" card. What occurs in the past is only there to show why the "You Now" came to be what it is. Similarly, the cards in the future are there to indicate where things are heading, based on the way things are in the present.

3. THE SPREAD'S FOCUSES   The story line in the spread actually represents the player, but the three focuses that make up the line ("Old Focus," "The Issue," and "New Focus") do not necessarily describe the player himself. These are *focuses of attention* regardless of whether they are facets inside or outside oneself. They do not need to be seen as hard and fast parts of reality, but their reality is certainly real in that one's attention is fixed on them. The terms "focus" and "issue" are almost interchangeable.

4. THE "HELPING" AND "DISTRACTING" CARDS
These two cards refer to the present and are not directly related to past or future. Also, they are often confusing to the player, sometimes paradoxical in nature. There may be occasions when it seems that the symbols in these two boxes should be switched, the "Helping" symbol seen as "Distracting" and vice versa. Often the process of Picture Stories helps the player understand the real role of these symbols in relation to his or her topic.

5. "THE ISSUE" AND "YOU NOW" CARDS   These symbols are the key to the rest of the Sky Spread, the core of the information available to the player. Every effort should be made to work with these symbols in the clearest way possible. In doing so, watch for how the two symbols interact in the Picture Story process. Does the "You Now" act on "The Issue" or the other way around? Do they avoid each other or confront each other? During the Best Picture part of the process, try to see that the "You Now" symbol actually does confront and deal with "The Issue symbol." The picture of that action will serve as the blueprint for successfully dealing with the actual situation.

6. MAKING PICTURE STORIES   Doing this part of the process can seem difficult at first. The key is to actually imagine a *picture* in one's mind using the group of symbols. Often it is such an instantaneous grouping of images that the player is hardly aware he has formed a picture. Or it is one so simply conceived that the player discards it, thinking there is something better to find. It is exactly those immediate pictures, though, that are the most accurate and revealing.

Try always to stay with just the simple symbols involved, adding no other elements to the picture. The one exception is oneself, especially when the symbols all seem inanimate. In these cases, it is quite permissible to insert oneself into the picture in order to put it all together.

Working with Stars in Picture Stories can seem more difficult than with other symbols, especially when more than one Star is involved. When there is such difficulty, try looking back to the card's word side. Imagine the word that describes the Star's energy as creating a certain kind of atmosphere around the other symbols involved. Or imagine the being described on the card—for example, "The Doer"—as actually present in the picture but invisible. When there are two or more Stars in a Picture Story group, try imagining either the mix of atmospheres in one place or the imaginary beings together, each wanting its own way.

USING **STAR + GATE** WITH OTHERS

I nvolving other people when you use STAR + GATE can greatly increase its benefit to you. It is both interesting and rewarding to share what you see, feel, and experience. You may be surprised to learn other people's perceptions of the symbols as they relate to your topic.

Try going through the process of interpretation, telling the other person what you are experiencing at each step. As you go, let the other person share what he or she sees. Watch for those places where you have the same perceptions and for those where they differ.

You might also choose to explore your relationship with another person, or a decision that affects both of you, or a problem that you face together. You can also use STAR + GATE twice, first from your point of view and then from theirs.

However you choose to do it, involving others can add a rich dimension to the process as well as the ways STAR + GATE can work in your life.

CARD
INFORMATION

● ▲ ✦ ▼ ✗ ◣ ■

PREFACE

The preceding material showed how to use the Symbolic Cards in the Sky Spread and how to interpret the symbols for investigating personal topics. This section provides further explanations of each card, one per page.

The text makes reference to the symbols' positions within the Circle Pattern, which is described in more detail later in the book. Numbers and letters in the text refer to positions or areas on the circle; quotation marks and all capital letters, to keywords of the cards.

This section begins with a discussion of Card Types, the seven levels within the STAR + GATE system. The categories into which the cards are grouped are significant in themselves. Card Types represent dimensions of experience, such as "mood," "challenge," "talent," and so on. How these levels fit into the complete person becomes clearer as you become more familiar with STAR + GATE and as you learn about the Circle Pattern.

THE SEVEN CARD TYPES

THE STAR CARDS–
ENERGIES
A through L

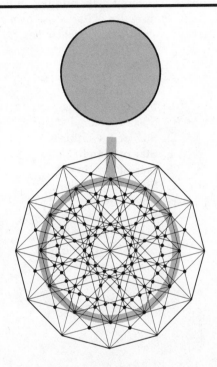

The Stars represent Consciousness in Energy. These are archetypal aspects of all beingness so pervasive in living that only such terms as light, energy, or moods can describe them and their effects in our lives. They are profound yet elusive qualities, ranging from noticeable outbursts of activity to energies so passive they seem not to be present.

The ring of Stars is the outermost labeled points on the Circle Pattern, shown in bright yellow. Within their ring lie all the other named points on the Circle (1-84). In great part, it is the intermingling of the Star energies that creates the particular symbols at the other intersections. Their web of light symbolizes the very fabric of our existence.

Each Star card carries the name of an imaginary being on the card's word side. This being typifies the kind of energy involved. A boldfaced word below the name also describes the kind of mood or atmosphere the card symbolizes.

Each Star is situated in such a way on the circle that it is shared between two Houses. Its energy plays an integral part in expressing the qualities of its Houses. Each Star is also over a Sea area and, again, is essential in describing a particular Sea.

STARS (A–L)

A. Star of Impulse
B. Star of Reaching
C. Star of Change
D. Star of Inwardness
E. Star of Laugh
F. Star of Bowing
G. Star of Indecision
H. Star of Hope
I. Star of Austerity
J. Star of Independence
K. Star of Aspiration
L. Star of Patience

THE STATE CARDS–
CONDITIONS
1 through 12

The State cards are Aspects of Form. They symbolize outer states, conditions, and environments that can be present in various situations. Like the world of form, these conditions can be both beneficial and detrimental, depending on how we perceive them and deal with them. The word side of each State card lists both the advantages and disadvantages that can be involved with a particular symbol.

On the Circle Pattern, the ring of State points lies just within the ring of the Stars. There is one State point at the top of each Garden area in each House; it describes the inherent condition that goes with the House.

Each State point has two Stars next to it on the Circle Pattern.

The energies of these two Stars mix together to create the particular State. In a sense, these energies lock together to create a form or condition much in the same way positive protons and negative electrons attract and revolve around each other in the structure of the atom, the basic building block of the material world.

STATES (1–12)

1. Sand
2. Lightning
3. Rain
4. Mud
5. Fire
6. Water
7. Earth
8. Thunder
9. Snow
10. Fog
11. Air
12. Pool

THE STAR-CROSS CARDS–
SELF-EXPRESSIONS
13 through 36

The Star-cross cards are Aspects of Self-expression, ways for showing ourselves to the world. Each card describes a character, a side of oneself, that may be at play in a particular situation. Each character has several words associated with it. Each shows a way the character might be seen, depending on the viewpoint. For example, the Lover can be a giving and intimate role, but it could be perceived by another as being possessive and demanding. Each Star-cross shows the pluses and minuses of ways we can express ourselves.

On the Circle Pattern, the Star-crosses are the double ring of twenty-four orange-colored points. There are two Star-cross points in each House, on either side of the upper portion of the

Garden area. There are also two of these types of points near the top of each Sea area. Each Star-cross symbol is an expression of the qualities of both the House and Sea it is in.

The Star-cross points are the only points on the Circle Pattern that have unequal amounts of Star energies, as seen by the unequal lengths of the four yellow lines from a Star-cross to the Stars connected to it. The Star closest to the Star-cross point is the strongest ingredient in the symbol. The next closest Star is a strong but secondary ingredient, and the third and fourth are weaker influences by comparison. The text on the cards notes the two strongest energies for each Star-cross, listed in order of closeness to the point. It is the imbalance of energies that gives the Star-crosses, aspects of self-expression, their unique character among the STAR+GATE symbols.

STAR-CROSSES (13–36)

13. Magician
14. Lover
15. Child
16. Egg
17. Moon
18. Jester
19. Maiden
20. Butterfly
21. Knight
22. Swan
23. Sun
24. Monk
25. Wanderer
26. Tree
27. Chest
28. Glass
29. Duck
30. Leaf
31. Bell
32. Knife
33. Ladder
34. Window
35. Fountain
36. Candle

THE GIFT CARDS—
TALENTS
37 through 48

The Gift cards are Essences of Consciousness, representing talents, qualities, gifts of our essential nature that we bring to the world. These are some of the brightest, most vital facets of Self, facets that each of us has in full complement. The Gifts are not expressed as specific skills but as the underlying urge or inclination that may be exhibited in a variety of skills depending on the style of the individual.

Each Gift card has two (in one case three) steps, expressed by two words or phrases. The first word is the essential quality, which taken by itself could be overemphasized and thereby yield little of value. The second word describes the ability that can be achieved when the quality is brought out of oneself and developed in the world.

On the Circle Pattern, the ring of Gifts lies just within the ring of Star-cross points. There is one Gift in the center of the upper half of each Garden area. It is notable that the Gifts, being Essences of Consciousness, are the only points on the Circle where all three colors of lines—blue, green, and yellow—intersect; Gifts are a part of all levels of the circle.

GIFTS (37–48)

37. Root
38. Eye
39. Tunnel
40. Harp
41. Circle
42. Chair
43. Letter
44. Wheel
45. Wing
46. Tongue
47. Morning
48. Rope

THE KEY CARDS—
CHALLENGES
49 through 60

The Key cards, or Aspects of Realization, are a progression of challenges about inner and outer existence. How we are on the inside shapes what happens on the outside. How we deal with what occurs is the challenge. If we have actually created it, how do we treat it? Are we positive or negative? If we don't like what happens, can we accept responsibility for it? Can we take advantage of life's challenges, *transform* our perspective, and achieve realizations about ourselves and life?

Each Key card has four words associated with it. These are like a barometer against which we can measure our ability to address the particular challenge presented. The first two words on the card typically describe the apparent negative aspect of the symbol by which we tend to feel at the mercy of something. But when we can see what the symbol actually has to offer and how we can use it, then we cross the line. We begin to transform it into something positive and beneficial. So the last two words refer to the other side of the coin, to how the symbol can be transformed, *in terms of our perception,* into a realization. In each case, the challenge is to realize the power of personal perception, then to make real what is possible. Because the Keys refer to a process, the words "challenge" and "realization" are both used to describe them.

On the Circle Pattern, the ring of purple Key points lies just within the ring of Gifts and outside the ring of Gates. The Key point lies at the center of the figure-eight shape of the Garden area. It represents the place where the inner and outer worlds meet, where our inner outlook confronts the material world.

KEYS (49–60)

49. Cup
50. Rose
51. Powder
52. Serpent
53. Chain
54. Robe
55. Gate
56. Wind
57. Mask
58. Block
59. Wand
60. Ring

THE GATE CARDS—
ATTITUDES
61 through 72

The Gate cards, or Aspects of Mind, represent the ways we channel and direct energy through inner postures—attitudes, approaches, and beliefs. On the Circle Pattern, the ring of Gate points can be seen as the doorways into the circle's most interior ring, the Hall of Signs with its twelve Sign points. The Gate points are near the base of the Garden structure, and each Gate is shared between two adjacent Houses. They appear to link all the Gardens together around the circle. In addition, there is a Gate at the base of each Sea area, acting as a way in and out of the Sea. These Aspects of Mind, then, create essential connections throughout the basic areas of the Circle Pattern.

Each Gate card contains two words or phrases that describe its special function within our inner landscape. The words are paired approaches, like two sides of a coin, like a gate that swings in both directions. The important thing to remember about the Gates is that the two words or phrases denote facets that are needed in balance, each requiring the other to maintain harmony. It is the *combination* of approaches that make the symbol a viable Gate, or mind aspect.

GATES (61–72)

61. Tower
62. Glove
63. Ice
64. Stone
65. Hole
66. Sword
67. Token
68. Handle
69. Rod
70. Cherry
71. Arrow
72. Siphon

THE SIGN CARDS–
FULFILLMENT
73 through 84

The innermost points on the Circle Pattern are the Sign cards, or Aspects of Fulfillment. This is the core of the area called the Hall of Signs, and the Gates or Aspects of Mind provide access to them on the circle. Each Sign point lies at the "base" of a Garden; each point represents the inner sense of fulfillment that is related to its House as part of the cycle of growth.

Each Sign describes a way by which fulfillment is experienced. All of the ways described on the twelve cards are possible for anyone, but we tend to favor certain types according to our own styles and the kind of satisfaction we seek in particular situations.

SIGNS (73–84)

73. Mountain
74. Cake
75. Cross
76. Sea
77. Star
78. Lamp
79. Cave
80. Pearl
81. Coffin
82. Field
83. Crown
84. Key

THE NINETY-SIX SYMBOLIC CARDS

● ▲ ✦ ▼ ✗ ◗ ■

PREFACE

The following pages contain information about each of the ninety-six STAR+GATE cards. The pages are arranged in the order of symbols A to L and 1 to 84 and are therefore grouped according to Card Types as explained in the previous section.

Each symbol page has a heading with the card's number and name. The card's picture side is shown, which includes its name and symbol image. The word side is also shown, with the Card Type symbol and the keywords related to the image.

The text provided for each card (1) helps the STAR+GATE user better understand the concepts embodied in the keywords and (2) shows where the symbols fit into basic House and Sea areas (part of the universal Cycle of Growth) in the Circle Pattern.

THE STAR CARDS–
ENERGIES
A through L

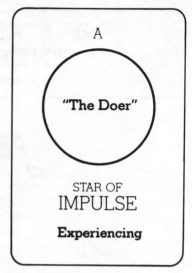

A. THE STAR OF IMPULSE

This Star's energy is all about do anything, be anything, try anything. It is typified by "The Doer," a being who does, and does,
and does. The energy is that of EXPERIENCING, regardless of
purpose, regardless of outcome, regardless.

The Star of Impulse is shared between the first and second
Houses. Therefore, the energy of "The Doer" is part of "I AM"
and "I WANT." It also creates the light of the Sea of Time (I).

On the picture side of this card, the Star's center shows energy
streaming out in all directions from a central point.

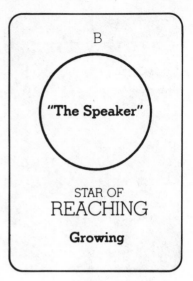

B. THE STAR OF REACHING

The Star of Reaching is about energy channeled in a specific direction, reaching for something. Behind this is the energy of "The Speaker," the being who encourages us to go and increase. The energy is that of GROWING, multiplying who we are and what we have. The Speaker is the timeless impetus to go beyond limitation.

The Star of Reaching is shared between the second and third Houses. Therefore, the energy of "The Speaker" is part of "I WANT" and "I RELATE." It also creates the light of the Sea of Innocence (II).

On the picture side of the card, the Star's center shows energy moving in a specific direction; the light from the Star is similarly channeled.

"The Mover"

STAR OF
CHANGE

Adjusting

C. THE STAR OF CHANGE

The Star of Change is about redirecting energy, the atmosphere of changing course. This is typified by "The Mover" who brings change by his very presence and through his every act. The energy is that of ADJUSTING, making way for change and progress.

The Star of Change is shared between the third and fourth Houses. Therefore, the energy of "The Mover" is part of "I RELATE" and "I FEEL." It also creates the light of the Sea of Birth (III).

On the picture side of the card, the Star's center shows energy moving at right angles to itself, denoting a change in direction.

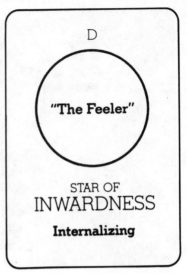

D. THE STAR OF INWARDNESS

The Star of Inwardness is about the energy experienced within oneself. It is typified by "The Feeler," the being who feels outside events on the inside. This is the energy of INTERNALIZING, of knowing one's emotions and inner drives, of taking things to heart.

The Star of Inwardness is shared between the fourth and fifth Houses. Therefore, the energy of "The Feeler" is part of "I FEEL" and "I PROJECT." It also creates the light of the Sea of Magic (IV).

On the picture side of the card, the Star's center shows a spiraling inward, creating a subdued outer light.

"The Player"

STAR OF
LAUGH

Externalizing

E. THE STAR OF LAUGH

The Star of Laugh describes exuberant, expressive energy, typified by the idea of "The Player" who can act out any role called for. This is the energy of EXTERNALIZING, vitality made visible.

The Star of Laugh is shared between the fifth and sixth Houses. Therefore, "The Player" is part of "I PROJECT" and "I BECOME." It also creates the light of the Sea of Laughing Hats (V).

On the picture side of the card, the Star's center shows energy spiraling outward, surrounded by bright, dancing light.

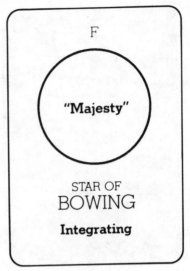

F

"Majesty"

STAR OF
BOWING

Integrating

F. THE STAR OF BOWING

The Star of Bowing combines the previous two Stars (D and E), acknowledging the value of each, blending in- and out-flowing into the energy of INTEGRATING. This is typified by the term "Majesty," the regal harmonizing of flow. It is that to which we bow in ourselves and in others.

The Star of Bowing is shared between the sixth and seventh Houses. Therefore, the energy of "Majesty" is part of "I BECOME" and "I INTERACT." It also creates the light of the Sea of Kings (VI).

On the picture side of the card, the Star's center shows energies moving in opposing directions, flowing through one another in balance, against a majestic light.

G. THE STAR OF INDECISION

The Star of Indecision describes the dance of energy that occurs between polarities. This vibration essential to all life is epitomized by "The Dancer," animated by dualities, creating a cosmic dance while WEIGHING the difference between two poles.

The Star of Indecision is shared between the seventh and eighth Houses. Therefore, the energy of "The Dancer" is part of "I INTERACT" and "I CARE." It also creates the light of the Sea of Music (VII).

On the picture side of the card, the Star's center shows energy swimming in two directions and a vibrating light issuing from the Star.

H. THE STAR OF HOPE

The Star of Hope is a passive energy, epitomized by "The Prayer," a being who waits for action to come from outside itself. The energy is TRUSTING, a faith in a higher or wiser source, a surrender of will.

The Star of Hope is shared between the eighth and ninth Houses. Therefore, the energy of "The Prayer" is part of "I CARE" and "I REALIZE." It also creates the light of the Sea of Pyramids (VIII).

On the picture side of the card, the Star's center is shown as receptive, expecting energy from outside itself; yet it emits a steady, secure radiance.

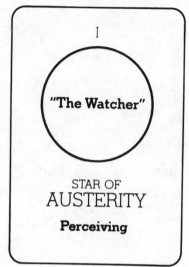

I. THE STAR OF AUSTERITY

The Star of Austerity denotes a cold, clear look. It is typified by "The Watcher," a being whose only task is to truly see. The energy is that of PERCEIVING, of finding what is really there and what is really going on.

The Star of Austerity is shared between the ninth and tenth Houses. Therefore, "The Watcher" is part of "I REALIZE" and "I PERFECT." It also creates the light of the Sea of Labyrinths (IX).

On the picture side of the card, the Star's center shows energy separated from a dot, or consciousness separating itself from an object, in order to truly perceive it.

J. THE STAR OF INDEPENDENCE

The Star of Independence is about nonattachment—to things or to people. It is typified by "The Deliverer," the being who releases ties and bonds. The energy is FREEING, loosening, making space.

The Star of Independence is shared between the tenth and eleventh Houses. Therefore, the energy of "The Deliverer" is part of "I PERFECT" and "I EXPAND." It also creates the light of the Sea of Quiet Flowers (X).

On the picture side of the card, the Star's center shows energy moving away from a point, or consciousness removing itself from something.

K. The Star of Aspiration

The Star of Aspiration is about transcendence. Typifying this is "The Seeker," the being who is always looking forward and looking beyond. The energy is that of DISCOVERING; the more you look, the more you find. It is not a matter of surpassing others but of transcending one's own views.

The Star of Aspiration is shared between the eleventh and twelfth Houses. Therefore, the energy of "The Seeker" is part of "I EXPAND" and "I MERGE." It also creates the light of the Sea of Stars Within (XI).

On the picture side of the card, the Star's center shows energy, or consciousness, rising up and out of its own light.

"The Dreamer"

STAR OF
PATIENCE

Imagining

L. THE STAR OF PATIENCE

The Star of Patience is the energy of ideas, or the idea of having energy. Typifying this is "The Dreamer," the being who dreams of the possibilities and potentials of all that could be. The energy is that of IMAGINING, to dream the dream, to sprout the idea.

The Star of Patience is shared between the twelfth and first Houses. Therefore, the energy of "The Dreamer" is part of "I MERGE" and "I AM." It also creates the light of the Sea of Dreams (XII).

On the picture side of the card, the Star's center shows swirling activity, much going on but undefined, radiating a quiet but dynamic light.

THE STATE CARDS–
CONDITIONS
1 through 12

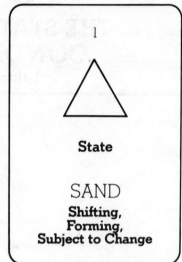

1. THE SAND

The Sand symbolizes the subtle condition of readiness, a kind of SHIFTING, like looking for footing. It is also FORMING, taking shape, making forms out of itself. The Sand, though, is moved by other elements, so its forms are SUBJECT TO CHANGE, rearrangement, even to being scattered.

The Sand is in the House of the First Cause (I), and it represents a mixing of the Stars of Patience and Impulse. Therefore, the Sand is the condition of "I AM," an outgrowth of the energy of IMAGINING combining with EXPERIENCING.

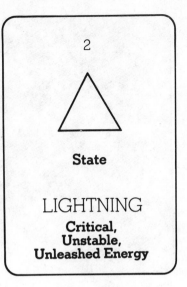

2

State

LIGHTNING

Critical,
Unstable,
Unleashed Energy

LIGHTNING

2. THE LIGHTNING

The Lightning is a condition that is CRITICAL, one that seems to border on chaos yet is loaded with energy. It is a condition that is UNSTABLE; something is bound to happen, but no one knows where the lightning will strike. It is a state in which great amounts of ENERGY are UNLEASHED. What may have been static before is now undeniably dynamic and powerful.

The Lightning is in the House of the Matrix (II), and it represents a mixing of the Stars of Impulse and Reaching. Therefore, the Lightning is the condition of "I WANT," an outgrowth of the energy of EXPERIENCING combining with GROWING.

State

RAIN

**Renewal,
Release,
Emotional**

3. THE RAIN

The Rain is a condition that washes away the old; it brings RENEWAL, a break followed by a fresh beginning. It prompts RELEASE, a freeing, a loosening up. It is also an EMOTIONAL condition, where feelings find expression.

The Rain is in the House of the Motion (III), and it represents the mixing of the Stars of Reaching and Change. Therefore, the Rain symbolizes the condition of "I RELATE," an outgrowth of the energy of GROWING combining with ADJUSTING.

4

State

MUD

Complex,
Immobile,
Fertile

4. THE MUD

The Mud is a state where things seem to come to a halt. It symbolizes a COMPLEX condition, with much to consider. It is more or less static, IMMOBILE, not going anywhere. It is also a FERTILE state, a condition that nurtures new growth or reevaluation.

The Mud is in the House of the Pure Water (IV), and it represents the mixing of the Stars of Change and Inwardness. Therefore, the Mud is the condition of "I FEEL," an outgrowth of the energy of ADJUSTING combining with INTERNALIZING.

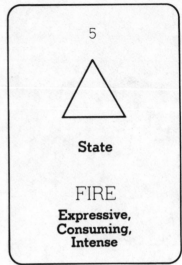

State

FIRE

**Expressive,
Consuming,
Intense**

5. THE FIRE

The Fire symbolizes a volatile condition. It is at once EXPRESSIVE and outgoing yet CONSUMING, exacting its toll. It is an IN-TENSE state, whether it reflects the heat of battle or that of passion.

The Fire is in the House of the Spirit Incarnate (V), and it represents the mixing of the Stars of Inwardness and Laugh. Therefore, the Fire is the condition of "I PROJECT," an outgrowth of the energy of INTERNALIZING combining with EXTERNAL-IZING.

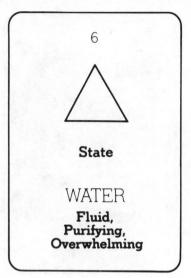

6. THE WATER

The Water is a state that is FLUID, bending, being open and receptive. Its condition is one of PURIFYING, cleansing old wounds. The Water can also be OVERWHELMING, a condition in which one could drown or be swept away.

The Water is in the House of the Grand Plan (VI), and it represents the mixing of the Stars of Laugh and Bowing. The Water symbolizes the condition of "I BECOME," an outgrowth of the energy of EXTERNALIZING combining with INTEGRATING.

State

EARTH

Resources,
Stability,
Structured

7. THE EARTH

The Earth as a condition symbolizes RESOURCES, the wealth of ingredients and possibilities at our fingertips. It is also a state of STABILITY, of being on firm ground. And it represents conditions that are STRUCTURED. Roles and ground rules are made apparent.

The Earth is in the House of the Perfect Union (VII), and it represents the mixing of the Stars of Bowing and Indecision. Therefore, the Earth symbolizes the condition of "I INTERACT," an outgrowth of the energy of INTEGRATING combining with WEIGHING.

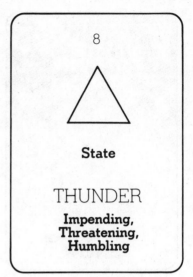

8. THE THUNDER

Distant thunder alerts us to a storm, and so the Thunder is an IMPENDING state—something is about to happen, probably something out of our control. It can be a THREATENING condition. What will happen? Will anything be destroyed? The questions hang in the air . . . waiting. The Thunder is also a HUMBLING condition. We realize our own smallness in the face of the bigness of the moving universe.

The Thunder is in the House of the Power (VIII), and it represents the mixing of the Stars of Indecision and Hope. Therefore, the Thunder is the condition of "I CARE," an outgrowth of the energy of WEIGHING combining with TRUSTING.

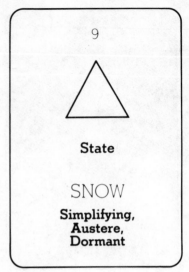

9

State

SNOW

Simplifying,
Austere,
Dormant

9. THE SNOW

A snow cover softens the landscape in a SIMPLIFYING gesture. It is a condition as stark as it is beautiful; things are reduced to black and white. The Snow is an AUSTERE state, cold yet clear. Under the Snow, conditions are DORMANT; life is frozen or hibernating, waiting for the new season to come.

The Snow is in the House of the Illumination (IX), and it represents the mixing of the Stars of Hope and Austerity. The Snow is the condition of "I REALIZE," an outgrowth of the energy of TRUSTING combining with PERCEIVING.

10

State

FOG

**Diffused,
Delusions,
Enveloping**

10. THE FOG

The Fog is a DIFFUSED condition, one in which borders are unclear, steering is difficult. It is a state of DELUSIONS; distance is lost, nothing is as normal, and everything is confusing. It is ENVELOPING. Once surrounded by fog, one feels lost in it and ruled by it.

The Fog is in the House of the Perfect Form (X), and it represents the mixing of the Stars of Austerity and Independence. Therefore, the Fog is the condition of "I PERFECT," an outgrowth of the energy of PERCEIVING combining with FREEING.

11. THE AIR

The Air is a FREEING condition, one unfettered by difficulties. It is a state of MOTION, free movement and intermingling. It is also UNLIMITED; the air sweeps the entire landscape without straining against other forces.

The Air is in the House of the Unification (XI), and it represents the mixing of the Stars of Independence and Aspiration. Therefore, the Air is the condition of "I EXPAND," an outgrowth of the energy of FREEING combining with DISCOVERING.

12. THE POOL

The Pool is a state of repose, a condition of REFLECTION and evaluation, a rest. It is a TRANQUIL state, without tension or stress. Yet it can be a STAGNANT condition of resting on one's laurels or being afraid to go forward.

The Pool is in the House of the Dissolution (XII), and it represents the mixing of the Stars of Aspiration and Patience. Therefore, the Pool is the condition of "I MERGE," an outgrowth of the energy of DISCOVERING combining with IMAGINING.

THE STAR-CROSS CARDS—
SELF-EXPRESSIONS
13 through 36

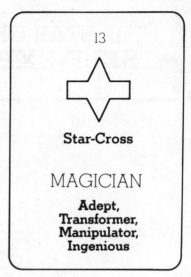

Star-Cross

MAGICIAN

**Adept,
Transformer,
Manipulator,
Ingenious**

13. THE MAGICIAN

The Magician is about that part of us that is ADEPT, knowing the world and how to work with the forces in it. As such, the Magician is a TRANSFORMER, able to bring about change, sometimes surprisingly. The Magician knows how to use his knowledge to his own ends and can be seen as a MANIPULATOR. In all, the Magician performs feats that few others can, and almost anyone would regard him as INGENIOUS.

The Magician is composed primarily of the Stars of Patience and Impulse, and it lies in the House of the First Cause (I). Therefore, it is expressing "I AM" through the energies of IMAGINING and EXPERIENCING. It is also an expression of the Sea of Dreams (XII).

Star-Cross

LOVER

**Giving,
Intimate, Possessive,
Passionate**

14. THE LOVER

The Lover is about the GIVING side of ourselves, an outflowing but INTIMATE side. At times the giving can become demanding; the Lover becomes POSSESSIVE and will not let the recipient go; it wants to cling. The Lover's pursuits are PASSIONATE, laced with zeal and a certain determination.

The Lover is composed principally of the Stars of Impulse and Reaching, and it lies in the House of the Matrix (II). Therefore, the Lover is expressing "I WANT" through the energies of EX-PERIENCING and GROWING. It is also an expression of the Sea of Time (I).

Star-Cross

CHILD

Innocence,
Curious,
Undeveloped,
Impulsive

15. THE CHILD

The Child symbolizes the part of us that is new and open—our INNOCENCE. The Child is curious; everything waits to be explored. It is also UNDEVELOPED, not fully grown or mature. And by nature, the Child is IMPULSIVE in its desires. What it wants comes first, regardless of what else is occurring.

The Child is composed principally of the Stars of Reaching and Change, and it lies in the Garden of the House of the Motion (III). The Child, therefore, is expressing "I RELATE" through the energies of GROWING and ADJUSTING. It is also an expression of the Sea of Innocence (II).

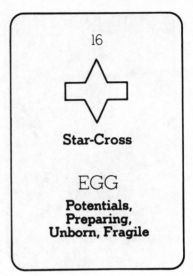

Star-Cross

EGG

**Potentials,
Preparing,
Unborn, Fragile**

16. THE EGG

The Egg describes the latent part of ourselves, the yet-to-be. It symbolizes POTENTIALS, expressing what we could become. It is what we are PREPARING in ourselves that is noticed by others—something that is as yet UNBORN. It is also FRAGILE in this condition; rough handling could change its fate.

The Egg is composed primarily of the Stars of Change and Inwardness, and it lies in the House of the Pure Water (IV). Therefore, the Egg is expressing "I FEEL" through the energies of ADJUSTING and INTERNALIZING. It is also an expression of the Sea of Birth (III).

Star-Cross

MOON

**Sensitive,
Longing, Magnetic,
Instinctive,
Moody**

17. THE MOON

The Moon is about our SENSITIVE side, one that is quiet and sometimes hard to read. It expresses a LONGING that is often undefined. It is MAGNETIC; others are drawn to it. Actions seem INSTINCTIVE, unexplainable but following nature. The Moon is also perceived as MOODY, emotional.

The Moon is composed principally of the Stars of Inwardness and Laugh, and it lies in the House of the Spirit Incarnate (V). Therefore, the Moon is expressing "I PROJECT" through the energies of INTERNALIZING and EXTERNALIZING, with an emphasis on the former. It is also an expression of the Sea of Magic (IV).

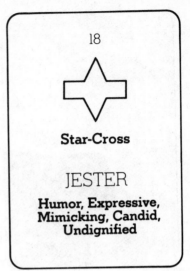

18

Star-Cross

JESTER

**Humor, Expressive,
Mimicking, Candid,
Undignified**

18. THE JESTER

Our lighter (and equally truthful) side is symbolized by the Jester. He has HUMOR; he is funny. He is EXPRESSIVE of what he thinks and sees. Often the Jester is MIMICKING the ways and roles of others. He is almost always CANDID in his appraisal of situations. The Jester can also be UNDIGNIFIED, untactful.

The Jester is composed primarily of the Stars of Laugh and Bowing, and it lies in the House of the Grand Plan (VI). The Jester's role is expressing "I BECOME" through the energies of EXTERNALIZING and INTEGRATING. It is also an expression of the Sea of Laughing Hats (V).

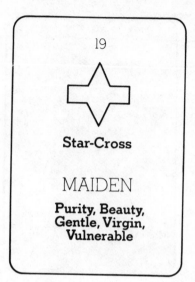

Star-Cross

MAIDEN

**Purity, Beauty,
Gentle, Virgin,
Vulnerable**

19. THE MAIDEN

Symbolizing our vision of PURITY and BEAUTY is the Maiden, the side of us that seeks the best for everyone. There is a GENTLE exterior. It is VIRGIN in that it is uncompromised and undebatable. And it is a side that can seem VULNERABLE to outside influences and to the wills of others.

The Maiden is composed principally of the Stars of Bowing and Indecision, and it lies in the House of the Perfect Union (VII). Therefore, the Maiden is expressing "I INTERACT" through the energies of INTEGRATING and WEIGHING. It is also an expression of the Sea of Kings (VI).

20

Star-Cross

BUTTERFLY

**Elusive, Delicate,
Emerging,
Carefree, Fickle**

20. THE BUTTERFLY

The Butterfly is about the rather experimental side of ourselves by which we attempt to act in new ways or transform old ones. It can appear ELUSIVE, something that is hard to get hold of. It is DELICATE as any new thing is. It is EMERGING, coming out in plain sight. The Butterfly is something CAREFREE, beyond limitation, and even FICKLE in its quest for new associations.

The Butterfly is composed primarily of the Stars of Indecision and Hope, and it lies in the House of the Power (VIII). Therefore, the Butterfly is expressing "I CARE" through the energies of WEIGHING and TRUSTING. It is also an expression of the Sea of Music (VII).

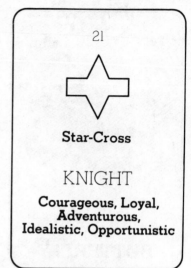

Star-Cross

KNIGHT

Courageous, Loyal, Adventurous, Idealistic, Opportunistic

21. THE KNIGHT

The Knight symbolizes the noble side of ourselves, that which is COURAGEOUS in its endeavors and LOYAL to its cause. The Knight is ADVENTUROUS and seeks new territories and kingdoms. It is IDEALISTIC, measuring others against lofty standards. At times the Knight is OPPORTUNISTIC, seeking personal gratification in the name of a great cause.

The Knight is composed principally of the Stars of Hope and Austerity, and it lies in the House of the Illumination (IX). Therefore, the Knight is expressing "I REALIZE" through the energies of TRUSTING and PERCEIVING. It is also an expression of the Sea of Pyramids (VIII).

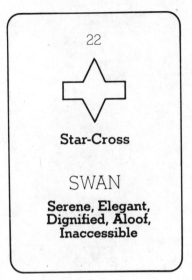

Star-Cross

SWAN

**Serene, Elegant,
Dignified, Aloof,
Inaccessible**

22. THE SWAN

The Swan is about our calm and together side. This is where one looks or feels SERENE, comfortable within. It is ELEGANT even if simple, and DIGNIFIED regardless of custom. Yet the facade can appear ALOOF, above the rest of the world and its troubles, or even INACCESSIBLE, driving away the interest of others.

The Swan is composed primarily of the Stars of Austerity and Independence, and it lies in the House of the Perfect Form (X). The Swan's role is expressing "I PERFECT" through the energies of PERCEIVING and FREEING. It is also an expression of the Sea of Labyrinths (IX).

Star-Cross

SUN

Radiating, Energetic, Vitalizing, Optimistic, Dominating

23. THE SUN

The Sun is the expansive and warm side of ourselves. It is RA-DIATING itself to the rest of the world. It feels ENERGETIC and is VITALIZING to those around it. As the "sunny side," it is the expression of OPTIMISM. Yet as a strong, outflowing force, it can also be a DOMINATING influence, seeking to have its way be *the* way.

The Sun is composed principally of the Stars of Independence and Aspiration, and it lies in the House of the Unification (XI). Therefore, the Sun is expressing "I EXPAND" through the energies of Freeing and Discovering. It is also an expression of the Sea of Quiet Flowers (X).

24

Star-Cross

MONK

Contemplative,
Humble, Profound,
Disciplined,
Sheltered

24. THE MONK

The Monk is about the philosophical and thoughtful side of ourselves. The Monk is CONTEMPLATIVE, pondering the nature and essence of things. In this pursuit, he is HUMBLE and often exhibits a DISCIPLINED life-style. His inner journey leads to actions or words that are PROFOUND and far-reaching in their impact. Some, however, will view him as SHELTERED from the everyday world.

The Monk is composed primarily of the Stars of Aspiration and Patience, and it lies in the House of the Dissolution (XII). The Monk, therefore, is expressing "I MERGE" through the energies of DISCOVERING and IMAGINING. It is also an expression of the Sea of Stars Within (XI).

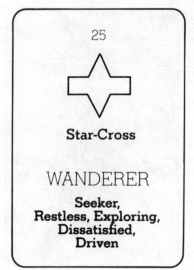

25

Star-Cross

WANDERER

**Seeker,
Restless, Exploring,
Dissatisfied,
Driven**

25. THE WANDERER

The Wanderer represents our searching side, that of the SEEKER looking for meaning, for purpose. It is a RESTLESS aspect, one that is constantly EXPLORING what the world has to offer. It is DIS-SATISFIED with the everyday and commonplace. The Wanderer is DRIVEN to satisfy an inner craving for answers.

The Wanderer is composed principally of the Stars of Impulse and Patience, and it lies in the Garden of the House of the First Cause (I). Therefore, the Wanderer is expressing "I AM" through the energies of EXPERIENCING and IMAGINING. It is also an expression of the Sea of Time (I).

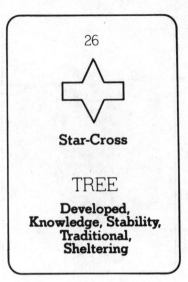

26

Star-Cross

TREE

**Developed,
Knowledge, Stability,
Traditional,
Sheltering**

26. THE TREE

The Tree describes the mature side of our nature, the part that is
DEVELOPED, grown-up. It is also a catalog of KNOWLEDGE
built up over time. It reflects STABILITY, having withstood the
test of time. It also describes a rather TRADITIONAL outlook,
having seen many things come and go. And the Tree, too, can be
SHELTERING to others, a place where rest can be sought in the
midst of a storm.

The Tree is composed primarily of the Stars of Reaching and
Impulse, and it lies in the House of the Matrix (II). The Tree,
therefore, is expressing "I WANT" through GROWING and EX-
PERIENCING. It is also an expression of the Sea of Innocence (II).

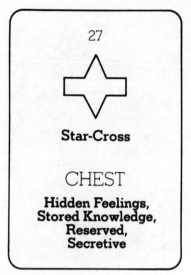

Star-Cross

CHEST

**Hidden Feelings,
Stored Knowledge,
Reserved,
Secretive**

27. THE CHEST

The Chest is about our reserved side, what is held back from the world. It symbolizes HIDDEN FEELINGS, emotions that are held in check for one reason or another. The Chest can also contain STORED KNOWLEDGE—that is, information that does not currently have a use. It is the part of us that appears RESERVED, not willing to do or say certain things. And it is a facet that can be SECRETIVE, holding something back from others.

The Chest is composed principally of the Stars of Change and Reaching, and it lies in the House of the Motion (III). The Chest is expressing "I RELATE" through the energies of ADJUSTING and REACHING, and it is the former energy that helps keep the lid on the energy of the latter. The Chest is also an expression of the Sea of Birth (III).

Star-Cross

GLASS

Reflecting,
Self-examination,
Clarifying,
Vanity

28. THE GLASS

The Glass (or mirror) is a symbol of our introspective side. It represents REFLECTION about who we are and what we are about. It is SELF-EXAMINATION, pondering our own motives, purposes, and behavior. The Glass can be a tool for CLARIFYING what we are all about, but the process can easily be seen as a kind of self-preoccupation or VANITY.

The Glass is composed primarily of the Stars of Inwardness and Change, and it lies in the House of the Pure Water (IV). Therefore, the Glass is expressing "I FEEL" through the energies of INTERNALIZING and ADJUSTING. It is also an expression of the Sea of Magic (IV).

Star-Cross

DUCK

**Naturalness,
Sense of Humor,
Conventional,
Self-doubts, Self-effacing**

29. THE DUCK

The Duck describes the part of ourselves that is CONVEN-TIONAL, going along with the way things are. To do so is to go with the grain, not against it, and so the Duck symbolizes a kind of NATURALNESS, being in step. It shows a SENSE OF HUMOR, that life does not have to be all seriousness. This same part of us can show SELF-DOUBTS, a nagging about one's own originality. It can also be SELF-EFFACING, doing things more for the sake of "the team" than for itself.

The Duck is composed principally of the Stars of Laugh and Inwardness, and it lies in the House of the Spirit Incarnate (V). Therefore, the Duck is expressing "I PROJECT" through the energies of EXTERNALIZING and INTERNALIZING. It is also an expression of the Sea of Laughing Hats (V).

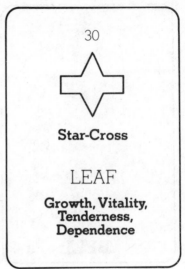

Star-Cross

LEAF

Growth, Vitality,
Tenderness,
Dependence

30. THE LEAF

The Leaf symbolizes the part of us that develops and increases; it
is new GROWTH, beyond what we were. Here we exhibit VI-
TALITY, a renewed spirit in our endeavors. It is also the TENDER-
NESS that accompanies a new shoot or budding blossom. And
there is a DEPENDENCE on those things that nurtured the new
growth.

The Leaf is composed primarily of the Stars of Bowing and
Laugh, and it lies in the House of the Grand Plan (VI). Therefore,
the Leaf is expressing "I BECOME" through the energies of INTE-
GRATING and EXTERNALIZING. It is also an expression of the
Sea of Kings (VI).

Star-Cross

BELL

**Attracting,
Attunement,
Alerting,
Heralding**

31. THE BELL

The Bell is about the part of us that is in tune with our world. Its own harmonizing is ATTRACTING, drawing others to it. It is ATTUNING—that is, vibrating between its sound and the other sounds around it, resonating to a common chord. The Bell calls. It is a side of us that can be ALERTING, warning of a danger, or HERALDING, announcing a significant arrival.

The Bell is composed principally of the Stars of Indecision and Bowing, and it lies in the House of the Perfect Union (VII). The role of the Bell is expressing "I INTERACT" through the energies of WEIGHING and INTEGRATING. It is also an expression of the Sea of Music (VII).

KNIFE

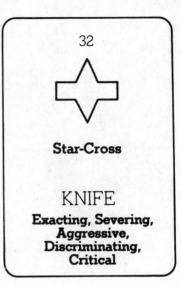

32

Star-Cross

KNIFE

Exacting, Severing, Aggressive, Discriminating, Critical

32. THE KNIFE

The Knife describes our critical side, where we find ourselves EXACTING about every detail, SEVERING ourselves from what does not suit us, and AGGRESSIVE in our posture toward others. The Knife represents expressing our DISCRIMINATING nature, our ability to be CRITICAL of others as well as ourselves. Here is the potential of being one's own worst enemy as a result of hard-lined stances.

The Knife is composed primarily of the Stars of Hope and Indecision, and it lies in the House of the Power (VIII). Therefore, the Knife is expressing "I CARE" through the energies of TRUSTING and WEIGHING. It is also an expression of the Sea of Pyramids (VIII).

LADDER

Star-Cross

LADDER
**Progression,
Success by Steps,
Achievement,
Ambitious, Zealous**

33. THE LADDER

The Ladder symbolizes the part of ourselves that seeks achievement. Here we look for progress, the PROGRESSION of events or circumstances. It is a forward-moving image of SUCCESS BY STEPS, moving up the ladder. As the nature of ACHIEVEMENT, the Ladder can serve as host to AMBITION, the need to get ahead, spiked by a ZEALOUSNESS in the pursuit of personal goals.

The Ladder is composed principally of the Stars of Austerity and Hope, and it lies in the House of the Illumination (IX). Therefore, the Ladder is expressing "I REALIZE" through the energies of PERCEIVING and TRUSTING. It is also an expression of the Sea of Labyrinths (IX).

Star-Cross

WINDOW

**Personal Viewpoint,
Observant, Perspective,
Separation,
Self-limitation**

34. THE WINDOW

The Window is about the side of ourselves that exhibits perspective. The Window represents one's PERSONAL VIEWPOINT that is expressed to others. It is a side that is OBSERVANT, trying to take it all in, in order to have PERSPECTIVE. The Window also describes a SEPARATION from the rest of the world, and the SELF-LIMITATION that can result from separateness.

The Window is composed primarily of the Stars of Independence and Austerity, and it lies in the House of the Perfect Form (X). Therefore, the Window is expressing "I PERFECT" through the energies of FREEING and PERCEIVING. It is also an expression of the Sea of Quiet Flowers (X).

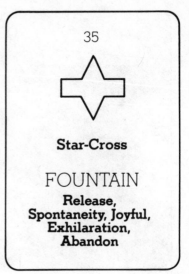

Star-Cross

FOUNTAIN

**Release,
Spontaneity, Joyful,
Exhilaration,
Abandon**

35. THE FOUNTAIN

The Fountain describes the joyful side of ourselves, which runs free and is self-inspired. It is RELEASE from tensions and worries, free to show SPONTANEITY of being, responding to life moment by moment. It is JOYFUL, a side that is filled with EXHILARATION, ready to do anything. The Fountain can also be ABANDON, a preoccupation with fun and a willful neglect of responsibility.

The Fountain is composed principally of the Stars of Aspiration and Independence, and it lies in the House of the Unification (XI). Therefore, the Fountain expresses "I EXPAND" through the energies of DISCOVERING and FREEING. It is also an expression of the Sea of Stars Within (XI).

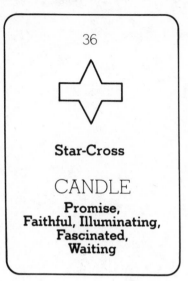

Star-Cross

CANDLE

**Promise,
Faithful, Illuminating,
Fascinated,
Waiting**

36. THE CANDLE

The Candle symbolizes the dedicated part of ourselves. It is PROMISE of the results and fruits to come. It is FAITHFUL to long-range affairs, plans, and goals. Its steady light is not great but it's constantly ILLUMINATING. The Candle is also watching the course of life with a FASCINATED gaze. And, too, it is passive, WAITING for events to shape the future.

The Candle is composed primarily of the Stars of Patience and Aspiration, and it lies in the House of the Dissolution (XII). Therefore, the Candle is expressing "I MERGE" through the energies of IMAGINING and DISCOVERING. It is also an expression of the Sea of Dreams (XII).

THE GIFT CARDS–
TALENTS
37 through 48

Gift

ROOT
**Source,
Connectedness**

37. THE ROOT

The Root is in the House of the First Cause (I) and is the Gift of "I AM." The Root, then, symbolizes the Gift of the emergence of anything—that it has a SOURCE, a home from which it came. Not only is this a symbol of an ultimate source, but also of having a heritage. This is the quality of feeling rooted, connected in time. This Gift's further achievement is CONNECTEDNESS, of being able to foster rootedness with others, of being able to make others feel comfortable and not estranged.

Gift

EYE

**Perceiving,
Vision**

38. THE EYE

The Eye is in the House of the Matrix (II) and is the Gift of "I
WANT." The most ageless of symbols, it represents the simple yet
profound gift of seeing. This establishes the basic construct of an
existence. The Gift of PERCEIVING requires a seer and the seen,
and speculation on who is the seer is a lifelong journey. Neverthe-
less, perceiving is that gift which opens the world to us so that it
may be known. VISION is a quality beyond perception—the gaze
that looks into things, both physical and nonphysical, in order to
truly *know.*

Gift

TUNNEL

**Inner Connection,
Accessibility**

39. THE TUNNEL

The Tunnel is in the House of the Motion (III) and is the Gift of
"I RELATE." This Gift is the product of the first two (37 and 38),
resulting in the ability to connect, inwardly and outwardly. The
Tunnel as INNER CONNECTION uses connectedness and vision
to "tunnel" within, tapping inner resources to assist in existence.
ACCESSIBILITY is the same talent focused outwardly, allowing
others access to the self.

40. THE HARP

The Harp is in the House of the Pure Water (I) and is the Gift of "I FEEL." It is the Gift of CREATIVITY in general, of being able to bring out, to give, what you feel. To express is one thing, to make a music of expression is still another. The achievement of this Gift, then, is HARMONY, to make a music that is heard as beautifully as it was conceived.

CIRCLE

Gift

CIRCLE

**Unity,
Participation**

41. THE CIRCLE

The Circle is in the House of the Spirit Incarnate (V) and is the Gift of "I PROJECT." It is the Gift of togetherness. If I am to project myself, there is nothing I would like more than to be in good company. The Circle is UNITY, the commonality of all things, all a part of a whole, and that Gift's achievement in the world is PARTICIPATION, every person acting like part of the whole.

42. THE CHAIR

The Chair is in the House of the Grand Plan (VI) and is the Gift of "I BECOME." This is the Gift of finding the right place. The Chair as POSITIONING is a sense of where things belong (for you). It is like walking into a room you have never seen before and knowing right away where you want to sit. This sense of what is appropriate can be brought out as a talent for ORGANIZATION and EVALUATION, not in the methodical sense but more of an instant recognition of workings.

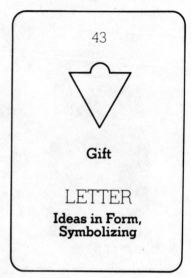

Gift

LETTER

**Ideas in Form,
Symbolizing**

43. THE LETTER

The Letter is in the House of the Perfect Union (VII) and is the Gift of "I INTERACT." This is the Gift of meaning within expression. Like a letter, the essential quality is the ability to express IDEAS IN FORM—that is, to translate thoughts into a medium. The translation is never perfect, though, because of the limits of the medium. So the real achievement of this Gift is SYMBOLIZING. This is the ability to imbue the translated ideas with meaning so that the message reaches *through* the medium to the perceiver.

Gift

WHEEL

**Experience,
Application**

44. THE WHEEL

The Wheel is in the House of the Power (VIII) and is the Gift of "I CARE." It is the Gift of getting your feet wet, of going through with things; the Gift of EXPERIENCE. It is the ability to go along with life and learn from it. The result of this is APPLICATION, knowing better what to do next time, having firsthand knowledge that can be applied in new ways.

45. THE WING

The Wing is in the House of the Illumination (IX) and is the Gift of "I REALIZE." The Gift of illumination is, truly, INSPIRATION, opening to all the potentials and possibilities that exist within us. This ability fully developed becomes LIBERATION; I see how free I really am, and I want others to have their freedom, too.

46. THE TONGUE

The Tongue lies in the House of the Perfect Form (X) and is the Gift of "I PERFECT." It is the Gift of actually getting something across—COMMUNICATION. The symbol of the Letter has to do with, say, finding the words. The Tongue has to do with finding the right words for the person you are talking to. So to bring out this most basic of Gifts, we learn the fine art of ARTICULATION, to be clear.

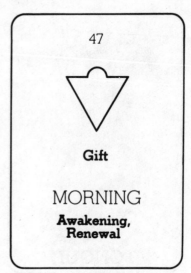

47. THE MORNING

The Morning lies in the House of the Unification (XI) and is the Gift of "I EXPAND." It is the Gift of a "fresh start tomorrow." The Morning as AWAKENING is our inherent ability to take a fresh look at things, whether after a night's rest or in the midst of deepest frustration, and realize there is another, simpler way to look at things. It is a nonrational Gift of perspective that has saved more than one life. And it is an ability that breeds RENEWAL; let's try again, tomorrow's another day.

48

Gift

ROPE

**Extending,
Effectiveness**

ROPE

48. THE ROPE

The Rope lies in the House of the Dissolution (XII) and is the Gift of "I MERGE." This is not, repeat *not,* the rope you hang yourself with. It is the Gift of EXTENDING, reaching out to others, the desire we have to assist, to go beyond ourselves. And its finest achievement is EFFECTIVENESS, finding out how to extend yourself in ways that work, for you and for others.

THE KEY CARDS–
CHALLENGES
49 through 60

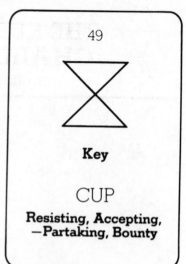

Key

CUP

Resisting, Accepting, —Partaking, Bounty

49. THE CUP

The Cup lies in the House of the First Cause (I) and is the challenge of "I AM." It is the realization about ownership; what I get in life does indeed belong to me. The Cup symbolizes how we deal with our lot, the cards we're dealt, our cup in life. I can RESIST the cup that comes to me, try to refuse it, accept no responsibility for it. Or I can passively ACCEPT my cup but worry about what is in it, feel victimized by it, even complain about it.

I can, though, cross the line of perception and see the Cup from a different point of view. I can PARTAKE of it. I brought it to myself; it must hold something especially for me. I can be nourished by it. Finally, fully meeting the challenge, I can turn my cup into BOUNTY. My cup is always there because I am creating it. What it holds is a bountiful return on what I am, on how I am being at any point in time.

The Cup is also the realization associated with the Seas of Dreams and Time (XII and I).

Key

ROSE

**Idealizing, Perfecting—
Unfolding,
Expressing**

50. THE ROSE

The Rose lies in the House of the Matrix (II) and is the realization of "I WANT." It represents the dilemma between *what* I want, *how* I want it, and the way things just are. The challenge is to realize the beauty of what is, and to be in step with the process of becoming.

The Rose is the question about perfection, about my inner sense of how things are *supposed to be.* When I am IDEALIZING, I am in a fantasy world of utter-perfection-according-to-me. I can't even really see you because you don't fit the fantasy. Or I can be a little more realistic. Now I'm only PERFECTING. You could be better; let me show you what's wrong. The trouble is, inside me, I'm not perfect. So everything that is not perfect in me, I end up seeing as imperfection in the world, and in you.

(continued)

(continued)

I can choose to see all this another way. I can see the whole thing as UNFOLDING, never quite perfect but always getting better. I can even see you in this new light. After all, you are dealing with your own sense of perfection, too. Better yet, I can let go of the idea of my being perfect and relax into EXPRESSING who I am and how I like things to be. Just being can be its own perfection, even if it's beyond me. This way, you get to be right, too.

The Rose is also a realization for the Seas of Time and Innocence (I and II).

51

POWDER

51

Key

POWDER

**Disintegrating,
Unforming,
—Transforming,
Creating**

51. THE POWDER

The Powder lies in the House of the Motion (III) and is the realization of "I RELATE." It symbolizes the impact of personal power in our existence; we can create, and just as easily destroy. It is the challenge of our treatment of other things, and of the results of that treatment. And, as such, it is the lesson of the responsibility that accompanies that most prized of freedoms—Choice.

Powder can be seen as DISINTEGRATING, our ability to wipe something off the map, or it can be seen as UNFORMING, coming apart, something reduced to its lowest common denominator. In the case of the latter, at least something remains from which something else can be made. We can cross the line into a more positive perception, though, and see almost a magician's Powder, which TRANSFORMS. Here we see the malleability of form based on one's approach to it. Finally, we step beyond to the Powder of CREATING, where the stuff of our existence is always the medium for self-expression.

The Powder is also a realization for the Seas of Innocence and Birth (I and III).

Key

SERPENT

**Instinct, Fearing—
Confronting, Knowing**

52. THE SERPENT

The Serpent lies in the House of the Pure Water (IV) and is the realization of "I FEEL." It represents the dilemma of the developing ego encountering its unknowable source and of confronting the inherent limitations of viewing life from a single point of view. The question of the Serpent is: How do I deal with what I do not know, with what seems beyond my control?

At the difficult end of the spectrum, we see the idea of the Serpent as INSTINCT—forces and mechanisms in the outside world that are acting on us. We can feel locked in an endless game of predator and prey. Inwardly, we can feel subject to our own appetites and drives; they can seem to run our lives. The step away from instinctive behavior is into FEARING. What I do not know and cannot control, I fear. But now, fear steers my course, not I.

I can, though, *turn* on my fear, face what I do not know, look into the eyes of the Mystery. CONFRONTING is *my* choice to change the nature of the game, to look at, to address what I do not comprehend. This leads to KNOWING. Shedding fear, I am no longer separate or out of control. The encounter is awareness, in and of itself.

The Serpent is also the realization for the Seas of Birth and Magic (III and IV).

53

Key

CHAIN

**Restraining,
Commitment—Relating,
Integrating**

53. THE CHAIN

The Chain lies in the House of the Spirit Incarnate (V) and is the realization of "I PROJECT." It is the challenge of commitments, of how we deal with the results of projecting ourselves into the world. We make links, ties with others, in order to have a footing for self-expression. The effects of those links is the dilemma presented by the Chain. It concerns more than just our relationships; it is all the ways we make commitments in the search for understanding and agreement.

The Chain can feel RESTRAINING, feeling bound by ties and commitments and wanting to break free. Or it can represent the hard end of COMMITMENT. *I said I would,* and I will! Even if I hold it against you later.

The other side of the coin is commitments connect me. We agree, therefore we can agree. The Chain gives me the basis for RELATING to others. A step farther brings an even better perspective—INTEGRATING. You are trying to establish links to the world, and so am I. In that way we are identical, acting like links in a chain. We make our essential links through small commitments, one leading to the next, in order to function in the world. Through the symbol of the Chain, we see that our process is intertwined with others, even though we may not always recognize it.

The Chain is also the realization for the Seas of Magic and Laughing Hats (IV and V).

Key

ROBE

**Roles, Specialization—
Character, Self-esteem**

54. THE ROBE

The Robe lies in the House of the Grand Plan (VI) and is the realization of "I BECOME." The question is this: Of all that I could do, what will I do, and how will I feel about it? This is not only a symbol of vocation or career, but also of all the ways we adopt roles and the extent to which we find self-esteem in them.

The Robe as ROLES represents our choices of ways to act in situations, whether a momentary role or a thread that runs through a lifetime. Role-playing can compromise the multifaceted self, yet every situation seems to require from us a stance. Out of the many role possibilities comes SPECIALIZATION. Certain roles are emphasized and developed, and we become a cast of characters, each with its special skill (and, perhaps, limitation).

Yet my selection of that cast of characters is unique to me; it reflects my CHARACTER, my style. The more I expose and develop each of those parts of me, the more each facet becomes balanced, well-rounded, and integrated within me, and this leads to SELF-ESTEEM. The Robe at its best can be seen as the ability to shepherd each of my roles as though they were my own children—none perfect, all loved.

The Robe is also the realization for the Seas of Laughing Hats and Kings (V and VI).

55

GATE

55

Key

GATE

**Opportunity, Indecision
—Entering, Discovery**

55. THE GATE

The Gate lies in the House of the Perfect Union (VII) and is the realization of "I INTERACT." It represents the question of how we deal with opportunity. Presented with the chance to go beyond where we are, we must deal with the not-yet-known as well as the potential of leaving something behind. The Gate is the challenge of interacting with the environment and with others. The question is this: Will I really go through the door?

Encountering the Gate, we know we have encountered OPPORTUNITY. But we don't know what is on the other side or where it will lead. We don't know if it is positive or negative, what we will gain or lose. Faced with such questions, we sit in INDECISION, contemplating the pros and cons of what *might* lie beyond.

The dilemma remains, and will always remain, until we take one simple deliberate step—ENTERING. We will never know until we do it, and once we do it, everything changes. We are no longer stuck; we are moving into something new and unknown. Beyond that is only DISCOVERY, experiencing what we entered. We will always enlarge our landscape as a result of addressing the challenge of the Gate.

The Gate is also the realization for the Seas of Kings and Music (VI and VII).

Key

WIND

**Dispersing, Changing—
Adapting, Directing**

56. THE WIND

The Wind lies in the House of the Power (VIII) and is the realization of "I CARE." The Wind symbolizes the lesson of give and take. The challenge is one of dealing with exterior forces and energy. To meet the challenge we must learn to shape our caring to the way the world really is.

When the Wind's energy rules and can blow away what I have made, its effect is felt as DISPERSING. When I learn that its effect is not against me, I begin to see its effect as CHANGING and respect the ebb and flow of things. The true changeover occurs when I alter my stance to the Wind and begin ADAPTING. This force outside of me is not going away; I can learn to get along with it, to adapt. Since it is a force, it can be harnessed. I can learn the art of DIRECTING the Wind, using its energy to take me where I want to go, remembering, though, that the essence of the force has not changed—only my approach to it.

The Wind is also the realization for the Seas of Music and Pyramids (VII and VIII).

Key

MASK

**Self-image, Hiding—
Self-acceptance,
Individuality**

57. THE MASK

The Mask lies in the Garden House of the Illumination (IX) and
is the realization of "I REALIZE." It represents the challenge of
discovering who I really *am* and what I *really* think of me.

The Mask is my SELF-IMAGE, the me I think I am when I look
in the mirror *and* when I address you. It is the "clothes" I wear out
in the world. But there is more to me than that, and sometimes I
find that the real me is HIDING behind that facade, unwilling to
come forth. Why? Well, I'd like to say it's because I don't trust
you, but I'm afraid the real reason is that I don't trust those parts
of me.

The resolution of the dilemma is to face all of me, what I like
and don't like about myself. This leads to SELF-ACCEPTANCE,
a different perspective on myself, devoid of inner judgments.
Without those judgments, I can perceive my INDIVIDUALITY,
and even my own *mask* is a facet of that uniqueness, the undu-
plicatable me. The process, though, never seems to be quite over.

The Mask is also the realization for the Seas of Pyramids and
Labyrinths (VIII and IX).

BLOCK

58

Key

BLOCK

**Obstacle, Problem—
Foundation, Building**

58. THE BLOCK

The Block lies in the House of the Perfect Form (X) and is the realization of "I PERFECT." The challenge on the path of perfection is dealing with all the things along the road that get in the way.

The Block perceived as an OBSTACLE stands in my way, stops my forward progress. If I look at the same Block in a slightly different light, it can appear as a PROBLEM. Now it is something that must be figured out, solved, before I can go on.

But I can cross the subtle line of perception and see the Block as FOUNDATION, a footing, a stepping-stone. Now the Block is not in my way; it is there to be used. And, further, I can see the Block as BUILDING, something to build with, or blocks as stepping-stones ahead of me. The question always is: When is an impediment a pediment? The answer is: When I say so.

The Block is also the realization for the Seas of Labyrinths and Quiet Flowers (IX and X).

WAND

59

Key

WAND

**Imagining, Potentials—
Will, Actualizing**

59. THE WAND

The Wand lies in the House of the Unification (XI) and is the realization of "I EXPAND." It is the challenge of actually doing something with one's ideas. On the road to wholeness, the closer I get the more my mind swells with promise. The question is: Will I do anything about it? Where is the magic wand?

Therefore, at the beginning the Wand is IMAGINING, and just that—all that could be, if I could just get this thing to operate. Beyond my imaginings is real POTENTIAL. The dreams are valid; they are dreams of better ways and better times, for everyone, not just for me. As in the story of the three wishes, if they were granted, we know we would choose what is beneficial and lasting. Still, caught in POTENTIALS, I can't make this thing work! What's wrong? Why won't someone help me?

(continued)

(continued)

The trouble with genuine ideas is this: No one knows what they are made of but me, the person with the great idea. It's not a matter of making the Wand work. The Wand is the symbol of what I must do—WILL the idea into existence. It's my idea. Who can do my idea *for* me? Now the whole problem is turned around. I am ACTUALIZING, making it happen. The "wand" is me, the instrument for bringing ideas *out* into reality.

The Wand is also the realization for the Seas of Quiet Flowers and Stars Within (X and XI).

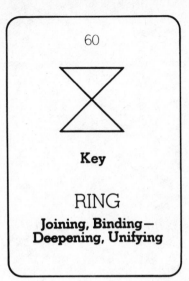

Key

RING

**Joining, Binding—
Deepening, Unifying**

60. THE RING

The Ring lies in the House of the Dissolution (XII) and is the realization of "I MERGE." It represents one's transcendence through union with another. Just as our journey will lead to discovering a complete universe within ourselves, so can we discover an equally rich universe within a relationship.

At the outset, the Ring is JOINING, like the ring of matrimony, a ring of friends, a bond. Yet the same Ring can become BINDING over time, or feel limiting, even suffocating at times. How can I overcome those feelings without breaking the Ring?

(continued)

(continued)

A relationship is an entity in which I participate. Realizing that I *control* a half of that entity and that I *affect* the other half of it, I can see the situation as an extension of me. I can approach the relationship as a living thing, and treat it accordingly. This is just one way of DEEPENING what the Ring (or relationship) can mean for me. Through this enhanced approach, I can reunite in the relationship. Now more than joining, I am UNIFYING the entity of which I am a part. In doing so, I am going beyond my personality to care for something larger than myself.

The Ring is also the realization for the Seas of Stars Within and Dreams (XI and XII).

THE GATE CARDS—
ATTITUDES
61 through 72

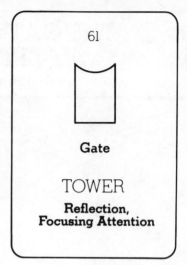

Gate

TOWER

**Reflection,
Focusing Attention**

61. THE TOWER

The Tower describes a dual aspect of mind that goes with the beginning and ending of the cycle of anything. A tower can be used as a high place from which to view all the surrounding landscape. In this respect, the Tower indicates gaining perspective, what the mind achieves through REFLECTION. This often goes with the ending of a cycle, the mind retreating to where it can see the whole picture and reflect on what has taken place.

From another point of view, the Tower represents FOCUSING ATTENTION, just as a tower can be seen as a single point of focus on the landscape. This is like the beginning of a cycle, with attention placed on something.

The balance desired is between being focused and unfocused. Each has its benefits; together they are harmonized.

The Tower is shared between the twelfth and first Houses and so acts as the gateway of "I MERGE" and "I AM." It is also the Gate to and from the Sea of Dreams (XII).

GLOVE

62

Gate

GLOVE

**Projecting Identities,
Accepting Assistance**

62. THE GLOVE

As PROJECTING IDENTITIES, the Glove is making our presence known in the world through the ways we can act. The Glove represents our personal collection of clothes, making ourselves visible through mini-identities that add up to a personality. Balancing this is the other side of the coin, ACCEPTING ASSIST-ANCE. The hand, once extended through the Glove, is met. The attitude here is one of meeting and receiving the extensions of others, of accepting what is offered for the sake of growth.

The Glove is shared between the first and second Houses and so represents the gateways of "I AM" and "I WANT." It is also the Gate to and from the Sea of Time (I).

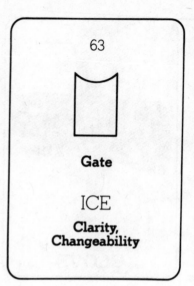

Gate

ICE

**Clarity,
Changeability**

63. THE ICE

The Ice symbolizes the CLARITY required to deal simply and effectively with the world. This clearness of mind streamlines one's efforts and dispels confusion. To keep that approach balanced, the Ice also represents CHANGEABILITY, a certain fluidity, knowing that a change of mind does not change the inherent validity of a being, just as ice does not lose its essential nature (water) should it melt. The same kind of clarity can still apply, but one that is tempered by changing climates.

The Ice is shared between the second and third Houses and therefore symbolizes the gateways of "I WANT" and "I RELATE." It is also the Gate to and from the Sea of Innocence (II).

Gate

STONE

**Steadfastness,
Integrity**

64. THE STONE

The Stone represents the STEADFASTNESS of mind that maintains a firm resolve amidst the currents of life flowing around us. To balance what could become sheer bull-headedness, the Stone also symbolizes a sense of inner INTEGRITY on which a firm approach is based. This is the integrity of what feels right within, and of acting in step with the model of oneself, true to an inner guide of how one should be.

The Stone is shared between the third and fourth Houses and so represents the gateways of "I RELATE" and "I FEEL." It is also the Gate to and from the Sea of Birth (III).

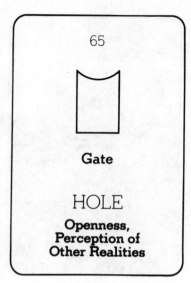

Gate

HOLE

**Openness,
Perception of
Other Realities**

65. THE HOLE

The Hole is about being receptive. The approach is one of OPEN-
NESS to all that is around you, receptive to the world's input. But
balancing this is an inner openness, receiving input from other
levels and dimensions of life, allowing PERCEPTION OF OTHER
REALITIES beyond the everyday and normal. These approaches
in combination lead to seeing the simultaneity of life, the intermingling of cause and effect, the wholeness of the moment and the
universe at large.

The Hole is shared between the fourth and fifth Houses and
therefore symbolizes the gateways of "I FEEL" and "I PROJECT."
It is also the Gate to and from the Sea of Magic (IV).

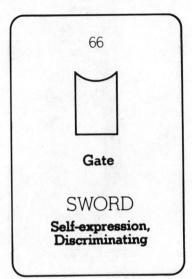

66

Gate

SWORD

**Self-expression,
Discriminating**

66. THE SWORD

The Sword symbolizes an attitude of SELF-EXPRESSION, of demonstrating who we are to the world through our acts. As a sword is an extension of the body, so is all that we do an extension of the self. To maintain balance with expression, the Sword also represents DISCRIMINATION, a sense of what is appropriate and what is not, as well as a sense of timing, an artfulness.

The Sword is shared between the fifth and sixth Houses and so represents the gateways of "I PROJECT" and "I BECOME." It is also the Gate to and from the Sea of Laughing Hats (V).

TOKEN

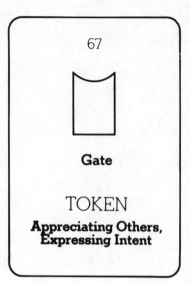

67

Gate

TOKEN

Appreciating Others, Expressing Intent

67. THE TOKEN

The Token is pictured as a nicely wrapped present, symbolizing the attitude of APPRECIATING OTHERS, acknowledging the role of others in your own life. But the Token also is about gesturing in another way, EXPRESSING INTENT. We use tokens and gestures of all kinds to let others know where we are and what we want. In combination, these two approaches are an outflowing of energy that carries information about the giver as well as the receiver.

The Token is shared between the sixth and seventh Houses and therefore symbolizes the gateways of "I BECOME" and "I INTERACT." It is also the Gate to and from the Sea of Kings (VI).

HANDLE

68

Gate

HANDLE

**Initiative,
Responsibility**

68. THE HANDLE

The Handle represents INITIATIVE, grasping opportunities as they come along. This is the attitude of starting things, not waiting for others to do it for you. Balancing this is the approach of RESPONSIBILITY, being responsive to, and responsible about, what comes as a result of initiative. One is reaching for the handle; the other is handling what you get.

The Handle is shared between the seventh and eighth Houses and so symbolizes the gateways of "I INTERACT" and "I CARE." It is also the Gate to and from the Sea of Music (VII).

Gate

ROD

**Command,
Discretion**

69. THE ROD

The Rod is about the force and impact the mind has on the world. When clear and purposeful, it carries the approach of COMMAND in the simplest and most direct sense: by my word, by my will. A compelling thrust beyond debate, above criticism. Yet the Rod can also mete out justice. So the balancing approach is one of discernment about how such command is used, utilizing DISCRETION. In combination, the Rod is the force of the empowered will tempered by a sense of fairness and justice.

The Rod is shared between the eighth and ninth Houses and so symbolizes the gateways of "I CARE" and "I REALIZE." It is also the gate to and from the Sea of Pyramids (VIII).

CHERRY

70

Gate

CHERRY

**Getting Involved,
Inner Completeness**

70. THE CHERRY

The Cherry symbolizes following one's desires and feelings, allowing GETTING INVOLVED. Through this approach one seeks companionship, nurturing, even gratification. Balancing the approach of involvement is the Cherry as INNER COMPLETENESS—that is, the attitude of already being a complete entity, like a ripened fruit ready for harvest. In combination, seeking out others is balanced by an inner well-being.

The Cherry is shared between the ninth and tenth Houses and so symbolizes the gateways of "I REALIZE" and "I PERFECT." It is also the Gate to and from the Sea of Labyrinths (IX).

Gate

ARROW

**Decisiveness,
Spontaneity**

71. THE ARROW

The Arrow symbolizes the ability of the mind to show DECISIVE-NESS, to reach a conclusion and then to follow it. This being able to make up your mind is kept from being bogged down by SPONTANEITY. Here is the attitude that you can change your mind as freely as you originally made it up. In combination, the ability to choose and rechoose joins with the skill of steering a steady course of action once a decision has been made.

The Arrow is shared between the tenth and eleventh Houses and so represents the gateways of "I PERFECT" and "I EXPAND." It is also the Gate to and from the Sea of Quiet Flowers (X).

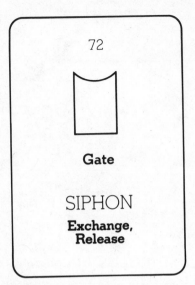

72

Gate

SIPHON

**Exchange,
Release**

72. THE SIPHON

The Siphon is essentially the ability of the mind to let go. As EXCHANGE, the Siphon is the approach of mixing energies with others without concern about the results. It is give and take with no scorekeeping. This allows truly combining with others. Along with this, the Siphon also symbolizes RELEASE, simply and truly letting go. This is the attitude of nonattachment, letting everything find its own place and its own level. In combination, the approach of nonattachment brings its own measure of exchanges; exchange need not be parasitic.

The Siphon is shared between the eleventh and twelfth Houses and so represents the gateways of "I EXPAND" and "I MERGE." It is also the Gate to and from the Sea of Stars Within (XI).

THE SIGN CARDS—
FULFILLMENT
73 through 84

Sign

MOUNTAIN

Fulfillment through Perseverance

73. THE MOUNTAIN

The Mountain is in the House of the First Cause (I) and represents the fulfillment of "I AM." The goal is one that must be mounted and climbed all the way to the top before one feels satisfied and finished. Such a high and single-minded goal requires PERSEVER-ANCE to make it to the top. What is difficult about this kind of fulfillment is that nothing short of the top will do. The dedication required sometimes shuts out valuable input along the way. Once at the top, one directed to this type of goal may see another, higher mountain that dwarfs his own.

74. THE CAKE

The Cake is in the House of the Matrix (II) and represents the fulfillment of "I WANT." This is the "goodie" card. To know I've made it, I want all the goodies. This is a tall order calling for MATERIAL REWARD, a return on all investments—with interest—and PHYSICAL SATISFACTION, complete with luxury, comforts, and pleasure. The Cake is no subtle hint about human preoccupations, yet each of us seeks our share of comforts and the stability of having resources.

75

Sign

CROSS

**Revelation,
New Direction,
Spiritual Awakening**

75. THE CROSS

The Cross is in the House of the Motion (III) and symbolizes fulfilling "I RELATE." The epitome of relating to one's existence is the gestalt of the sense of it all—REVELATION. Through such a profound experience, the Cross can open new pathways, providing NEW DIRECTION. This dawning realization of the wholeness and livingness of the universe is, indeed, SPIRITUAL AWAKENING.

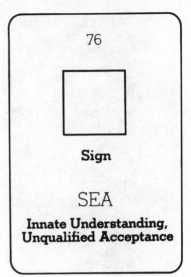

76. THE SEA

The Sea is in the House of the Pure Water (IV) and represents the fulfillment of "I FEEL." The Sea, ageless mother of life on Earth, symbolizes the state of timeless knowing, INNATE UNDERSTANDING. And the Sea loves each of her children with UNQUALIFIED ACCEPTANCE. The type of satisfaction demonstrated by the Sea is a complete and utter trust in the way of all things coupled with an unshakable inner knowing.

77. THE STAR

The Star is in the House of the Spirit Incarnate (V) and represents the fulfillment of "I PROJECT." This is that lofty brand of fulfillment whereby reaching for the stars, truly SEEKING, results in constant DISCOVERY. The aspiring soul, because it dares to reach and seek the heights, is rewarded with bountiful sights.

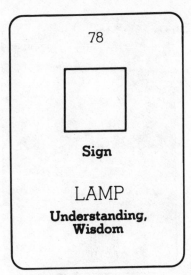

78

Sign

LAMP

**Understanding,
Wisdom**

78. THE LAMP

The Lamp is in the House of the Grand Plan (VI) and is the
fulfillment of "I BECOME." Becoming is the education and development of the self, breeding a conscious UNDERSTANDING
about the process of living. The fermentation of that precious fruit
is WISDOM, a knowledge that serves as a guide for others on the
path of their becoming.

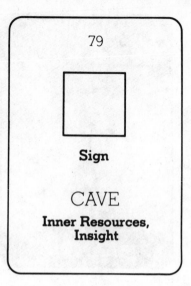

Sign

CAVE

**Inner Resources,
Insight**

79. THE CAVE

The Cave is in the House of the Perfect Union (VII) and represents
the fulfillment of "I INTERACT." The final, the ultimate interaction is within, with the seemingly unconscious parts of ourselves.
When this union within occurs, we find ourselves with vast
INNER RESOURCES that had seemed hidden before. And those
inner connections lead to a clearer vision of the world beyond
appearances; we discover INSIGHT, obvious and clear.

80. THE PEARL

The Pearl is in the House of the Power (VIII) and symbolizes the fulfillment of "I CARE." The Pearl is a precious substance formed slowly, day by day, through the process of nature. Here it is a symbol of enduring the test of time, of profiting from every win or loss, of having been there and back, resulting in a quiet confidence, a SELF-ASSUREDNESS that is gained from EXPERIENCE.

Sign

COFFIN

**Transformation,
Regeneration,
Rebirth**

COFFIN

81. THE COFFIN

The Coffin is in the House of the Illumination (IX) and represents
the fulfillment of "I REALIZE." This is the symbol of shedding
skins, of evolving beyond what one has been. It does not literally
mean death; it does mean TRANSFORMATION that results from
profound realization; REGENERATION, a new life rising out of
the old; and REBIRTH, major new starts from giant leaps in
awareness. Why the solemn picture of a coffin? The major shifts
in consciousness indicated by this card require putting old frame-
works truly to bed, but doing so with a reverence for the valid role
of the old ways in begetting the new.

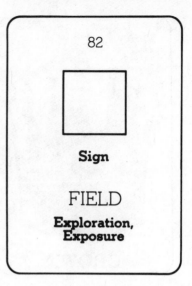

Sign

FIELD

**Exploration,
Exposure**

82. THE FIELD

The Field is in the House of the Perfect Form (X) and symbolizes
the fulfillment of "I PERFECT." This is the kind of satisfaction
that comes from *living out* realizations, for the world's benefit and
for your own. It involves EXPLORATION of how concepts, realized within, are actually and literally at work in the everyday
world. And it involves EXPOSURE, letting your true self be seen
and, in turn, being exposed to the variety of development around
you. Fame, toil, and service are intertwined in the Field of perfecting.

CROWN

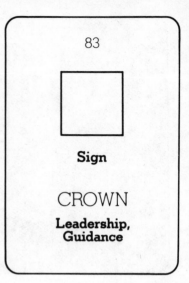

83

Sign

CROWN

**Leadership,
Guidance**

83. THE CROWN

The Crown is in the House of the Unification (XI) and symbolizes the fulfillment of "I EXPAND." Not the magician's hat or the general's helmet, the Crown cannot be sought or won. When it comes, it is bestowed; one finds one is wearing it. In proper leadership of my own life, I find I demonstrate LEADERSHIP for others. In pursuit of the right guidance for myself, I find that I convey GUIDANCE to those around me. It is by example that the Crown is earned, and then only for the sake of all concerned.

Sign

KEY

**Self-discovery,
Individual Realization**

84. THE KEY

The Key is in the House of the Dissolution (XII) and symbolizes the final fulfillment, that of "I MERGE." I find the Key and discover that it is me—SELF-DISCOVERY. The microcosm of my self is complete. Perfection is no longer an issue; to know all that I am is what matters. To be all that I can be, INDIVIDUAL REALIZATION is the Key. It opens me to all other selves and their quest. It brings me closer to that grander self from which I came, in which I dwell, for which I expand. I and thee and thou are one. That is the Key.

THE CIRCLE PATTERN

● ▲ ✦ ▼ ✖ ◪ ■

THE LIGHT

"The story of the light," he said,
"is in the dance of the Stars.
Look above you, in the sky.
All the universes spin within me;
all that I am is waiting for you;
and my song is in the dance of the Stars.

"Look in every direction, and you will see
the twelve Princes.
Their glory shines among you
though their home remains in my heart.

"Come out now, my son,
and take your place with me.
See the light within the light,
the mind within the mind,
step into the dance of the Stars
that is you."

Richard H. Geer

INTRODUCTION TO THE
CIRCLE PATTERN

After using the Symbolic Cards and Sky Spread to explore a topic, you can discover more about the cards you received by plotting their positions on the map of STAR+GATE, the Circle Pattern. By doing this you will be able to see relationships between the symbols that could not be recognized otherwise. Having the symbols translated into positions on the Circle Pattern reveals connections and relative positions leading to a clearer, more meaningful perspective on your topic.

The STAR+GATE Circle Pattern looks like a complicated web at first. Before using it, you need to understand how the various parts of the circle fit together and interact. The short introduction that follows will enable you to read the STAR+GATE map. After that, you will learn various ways to use the map. Finally, you will see how using the Circle Pattern deepened Ann's understanding of her topic and allowed her to see some surprising new meanings in her Symbolic Cards.

The Circle Pattern is dramatically different from the apparent simplicity of the Symbolic Cards, but it is important to know that the cards evolved from the pattern and not the other way around. To truly understand the cards and the overall sense of STAR+GATE, it is beneficial to be familiar with the Circle Pattern. Once you understand the way the circle is organized, it will serve as a ready reference for any of the deeper looks you may take at the symbols.

To begin with, imagine the circle as empty, no crisscrossing lines, just a center point and an outside edge. There are two enormous urges at work on the circle, the same two pervasive urges we feel throughout our lives. One could be called the urge to "go home," the other the urge to "stay out late." They are equal and opposite inclinations, each with its own validity at different times and in different situations. This can also be thought of as a creative tension present in almost every life situation.

The urge to "go home" is the desire to return to a source. Dorothy had that feeling about Kansas in *The Wizard of Oz*. The source is the beginning place, or wherever we were before we were here. This is what the center of the Circle Pattern represents. Wherever we may be in life, we are capable of feeling the urge to "go home," back to the center.

Balancing that is the desire to do more, to move away from the center, to "stay out late." This is the urge to go everywhere, do everything, know everybody. We can be anywhere in life, and suddenly this urge pushes us past old limits, toward the outside, beyond where we have been. Here we feel the desire to expand, whereas the opposite is to contract.

Neither of these pulls is inherently good or bad. Certain situations can make us feel one way or another. At times we experience a sort of push-pull: one part of us wants to go home, the other wants to stay out late.

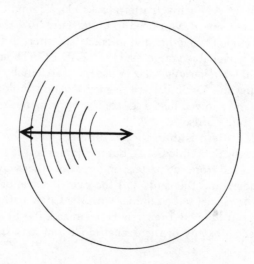

One urge pulls us inside to the inner universe, the other brings us out, a push into the outer world. From where we live, we don't know how far inside we can go, or how far outside. So the center and the perimeter of the Circle Pattern represent absolutes, extremes we don't really expect to reach in normal life. We are always somewhere between the two, and that is the part which STAR+GATE maps.

THE SEVEN LEVELS

STAR+GATE points out seven stages between the inside center and the outside edge of the circle. This provides a way to chart the integration of the physical and nonphysical realms and of expansion and contraction in life. Looking at the Circle Pattern, you can see rings of colored points that mark the circle at different levels. Each point represents a Symbolic Card, and the rings of colored points indicate the seven Card Types, or classes of symbols. The rings describe the spectrum of human awareness. The span is between the most deep-seated sense of fulfillment (the innermost ring of green Sign points) and the expansive, creative radiance of consciousness (the outer, light-yellow Star points). In between these rings are five other levels. These include the blue ring of Gates (the psyche's postures, attitudes, and approaches), the purple ring of Keys (confrontations, challenges that lead to realization), the pink ring of Gifts (unique qualities, talents, and abilities), the double ring of orange Star-cross points (ways of expressing ourselves out in the world), and the deep yellow ring of States (the conditions we can find ourselves in, the tools for discovery, progress, and even destruction).

THE COLORED LINES

Each line of color on the circle represents a different kind of connection; together, they spin a web of interrelationships between the circle's points, and, therefore, between the symbols themselves.

Having looked at the circle as empty, let's begin to add the lines, color by color. The blue Cloud lines emanate from twelve places on the edge of the circle, dividing the edge into twelve segments. These segments will give us a way to distinguish one part of the circle from another, like the difference between ten and eleven o'clock. The Cloud lines also create all the major divisions *within* the circle's area. If you look at pairs of parallel blue lines, you will see the outside limits of the twelve areas on the circle called Houses.

**CIRCLE'S
BLUE LINES**

Notice the long rectangles running across the circle made by blue lines and the outside segments of the circle. Each half of a rectangle, from the center out to the edge, is one House. Near the center of the circle, the Cloud lines converge, creating an inner area called the Hall of Signs. The House areas overlap one another around the circle, but each House can be located easily if you remember that the top of each House is made by the outer edge of the circle, the sides by the blue Cloud lines, and the base merges with the Hall of Signs at the center of the circle.

The Cloud lines represent the most subtle kind of connection on the Circle Pattern, connection through *concept*. This can best be likened to the mind's ability to make connections and associations, to have an unchecked flow of ideas, to literally conceive of connections.

**BLUE LINES
MAKE HOUSES**

Next we overlay the blue lines with the green and see what they add to the circle. There are two kinds of green lines.

Those that emanate from the circle's outside edges (where the blue lines begin) make large overlapping squares around the outer part of the circle. These are called Bridges, and they represent connection through *relationship,* a kind of arm-in-arm connection

**GREEN LINES
(BOLD)
OVER THE BLUE**

like brothers and sisters in a ring. The other green lines, those that pass through the circle's center, emanate from where the Bridges first cross one another. These green lines are called Lineage lines, also representing connection through relationship but, in this case, more that of parent and offspring than of siblings. The flow of the Lineage is toward the circle's center. In each House there is a central Lineage line, parallel to the outer blue lines of the House.

Finally, we add the yellow lines over the green and blue. Although the yellow lines add much of the visual complexity to the circle, they simply repeat the patterns already established by the other lines. Where the yellow lines start are large yellow points called Stars. You can see that the Star points form a circle within the main circle. This circle is turned slightly, which results in each House having two Stars and each Star being shared by two Houses. The Star points are located where the green Bridge lines cross within the sharp angles, or Vs, formed by the blue Cloud lines.

The Stars (cards marked A–L), as discussed in more detail under "Card Information" (see page 25), represent essential kinds of energy. The yellow lines that emanate from them are called Star lines. Within the ring of Stars lie all the numbered points represented by the Symbolic Cards (marked 1–84). Each numbered point, or symbol, is therefore a unique mix of emanations from the Stars connected to it.

**YELLOW LINES
(BOLD)
OVER GREEN
AND BLUE**

170

The blue Cloud lines provide subtle connection by *concept*, and they outline the basic areas of the circle. The green Bridges and Lineages add structure through connection by *relationship*, both around and through the circle. Now the Star lines, building on the foundation of the others, bring the map to life, providing connection through directly *experiencing*, of being, doing, and encountering in order to truly know ourselves and the world.

THE "CYCLE OF GROWTH"— THE TWELVE HOUSES

Together, the three colors of lines build the twelve Houses. As a series, the Houses describe a classic twelve-part "Cycle of Growth," a cycle all things go through from beginning to ultimate completion. The cycle is applicable to the development of an idea, the life of a person, the course of a relationship, the evolution of a culture, and so on. It applies to anything large or small, tangible or intangible, individual or collective.

The following list is an example of the cycle in terms of human growth, briefly going through the keywords of Houses I through XII like numbers on a clock face.

I.	"I AM"	An infant just is. It lives and experiences. Its consciousness, however simple, is the center of its universe.
II.	"I WANT"	An infant finds it has needs and learns to express them.
III.	"I RELATE"	The emerging person sees that there is a world to deal with, things to learn about and to communicate with.
IV.	"I FEEL"	He begins to discover himself, his own ways, styles, moods; interior experience.
V.	"I PROJECT"	He learns the art of self-expression, of playing roles and adapting to a world with others in it.
VI.	"I BECOME"	He adds to himself, develops, envisions careers, refines roles in the world.

VII.	"I INTERACT"	He makes connections with others, establishes relationships.
VIII.	"I CARE"	He discovers the power of uniting, the desire to be more and to understand the nature of things.
IX.	"I REALIZE"	He uncovers his own purpose and begins to see higher purposes for living, opening more to the world.
X.	"I PERFECT"	He improves himself and helps others to do the same.
XI.	"I EXPAND"	He sees beyond personality to a larger scheme, accepting limits yet reaping richer rewards.
XII.	"I MERGE"	He is complete, acts in step with the whole, and, in doing so, dissolves back into it. He is ready for a new "I AM" at another level of being.

Due to the overlapping nature of the House areas, it can appear difficult to find in which House a particular point lies. Finding the Garden area of a House simplifies this process.

The diagram on page 173 shows the area of one House and

GARDEN

Gold "Top" of House
Blue "Sides" of House

White Point Goes
with Name of House

STARS (light yellow)

STATE (dark yellow)

STAR-CROSSES (orange)

GIFT (pink)

KEY (purple)

GATES (blue)

SIGN (green)

outlines the interior Garden structure. The pair of parallel blue lines marks the outer limits of the House. Parallel to them is a green Lineage line running through the center of the House. At the top of that Lineage line is a point that is shown in white on the printed version of the Circle Pattern. This point is not labeled with a number or letter like the other points, and it represents the name of the House itself, such as "I. The First Cause." Below that point, on either side, are two Star points. Below them is a figure-eight in yellow lines, symmetrical to the green Lineage line. This figure-eight, outlined in the diagram, is called the Garden.

In the Garden area, the uppermost (outermost, on the circle) point is the dark yellow State point. Below it, on either side, are two orange Star-cross points. Just below and between them is a pink Gift point. Below it is a purple Key point, below that are two blue Gates, and finally, at the base of the Garden (nearest the circle's center), is the Sign point.

When you want to know which House a point is in, first determine which Garden the point belongs to. It is easy, then, to see which House the Garden is in. Simply follow the green Lineage line out toward the circle's edge where the Roman numeral for the House is shown.

There are two exceptions. Star and Gate points are shared between *two Houses*. While this may cause some initial confusion, it should quickly become easy to determine the two adjacent Houses to which these points belong.

The foregoing will give you the orientation needed to perform the Analysis by Houses presented later. What follows is a different way of looking at the pattern, in terms of areas called Seas.

THE TWELVE SEAS

The Seas were a discovery that came about after the original recognition of the Houses. More insight about one's symbols can be gained by having an understanding of the Sea a symbol is part of. The information below will provide the necessary background to do the Analysis by Seas described later.

When you look at the diagram of the circle with just the blue Cloud lines, you are able to see the twelve Houses and the Hall of Signs by seeing the *rectangles* the blue lines create. To recognize the Sea areas, you need only look at the same blue lines creating angular divisions—almost triangles—instead of boxes. Each of these angular areas—or *V*s—is one of twelve Seas around the circle.

The Houses can be thought of as the more masculine aspect of the pattern, and the Seas as the more feminine side, although these terms are used in a broad sense and are not meant to refer to differences in gender. More to the point, the Houses are territorial, visibly organized, and connec*ting,* whereas the Seas are connec*ted,* more simply organized, and act more as reservoirs within the system. One is more external, the other more internal.

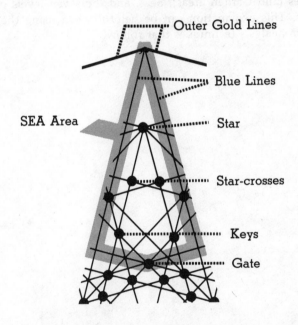

The Seas also describe the Cycle of Growth but in their own way. This cycle of the Seas is explained in the "Card Information" section. The order of the Seas is shown in the diagram on page 174; the twelfth Sea lies between the twelfth and first Houses. The Seas are numbered I to XII clockwise around the circle.

The overlapping of the Seas does not present the kind of complexity seen with the Houses, so there is no special name given to the interior structure of Seas, the points connected by yellow lines. It is on the tie-shape structure that the points relevant to a Sea are found. First, at the top of each Sea is a Star, whose particular energy can be thought of as filling the Sea area. Below the Star are two Star-crosses, side by side. Below them are two Key points, which also connect to the adjacent Seas. At the base of the Sea is a Gate point. This represents the way into and out of the area. (This is why every Gate point has two words or phrases that indicate paired approaches.)

That ends the geography lesson on the Circle Pattern, giving you a sense of how it is organized in terms of the Cycle of Growth, Houses (and Garden areas), Seas, and the seven levels or Card Types. This explanation can be helpful when using the Circle Pattern analysis techniques that follow.

USING THE CIRCLE PATTERN

This section explains four methods for analyzing symbols on the circle: Circuits and Analysis by Stars, by Houses, and by Seas. Each method is independent of the other, each reveals something different about your symbols, and you may select any or all of the methods depending on what kind of information you find of value.

The following pages show how to perform the analysis techniques with the two key symbols from the Sky Spread, "You Now" and "The Issue." However, the methods can be used with any of the other symbols in the spread.

CIRCUITS

Circuits is an analysis method that allows you to use the Circle Pattern to determine what other parts of yourself could be brought to bear in order to help resolve a particular topic. This technique will be especially helpful if you experienced difficulty in forming the Best Picture from the Sky Spread's Six-Step Process of Interpretation. Completing the Circuit, as described below, will give you one or more additional symbols to add to your Best Picture. This will result in a revised plan of action or approach that may be easier to understand and implement.

All of the points on the Circle Pattern represent parts of oneself. In truth, we all have all the parts at our disposal, but our individual styles and the situations that arise tend to emphasize certain qualities and not others. Circuits allows us to call on these other, less emphasized parts of ourselves for the benefit they can bring to specific situations.

To begin with, after using the cards and Sky Spread to explore a personal topic, check the number or letter of the two key cards in the spread, the "You Now" and "The Issue" cards. Find the corresponding letters or numbers on the Circle Pattern and mark these spots with a small coin or similar marker.

You can see that yellow Star lines flow through the two marked points. Star lines represent connection by *directly experiencing* (see "Introduction to the Circle Pattern," page 165), and each point has Star energies running through it. Look at the lines flowing through your two points to see if they are connected or not.

The two points are not usually directly connected by a *single, straight yellow* line. However, if they should be, this means symbolically that they are linked by a common energy, and that they are in a relatively harmonious position to one another. If this is the case, nothing additional is indicated with the Circuits technique.

Most often, the two points are not directly connected. Symbolically, this represents the situation that warranted your utilizing STAR+GATE in the first place. In most cases, the "You Now" and "Issue" are somewhat at odds with each other; plotting their place on the circle reveals a certain disconnectedness.

The map can help resolve that. Look along the yellow lines that flow through your two points. Try to find one point that could be added, the result of which would be a group of three points that connect up—like part of a circuit. There are cases where it may take two additional points to create a connected group of points. There are also cases when there may be several options. When you have choices, try to choose as few extra points as possible, and choose those points that correspond to symbols that you feel are the most fitting for yourself and your situation.

Symbolically, the extra point (or points) that makes a circuit with your two points represents a place where relatively divergent energies are brought into a harmonious *combination* of points. This means that the Symbolic Card corresponding to the point is a part of yourself that can help "You Now" deal with "The Issue."

To learn how to take advantage of this part of yourself, find the corresponding card in the deck and place it on the Sky Spread along with your "You Now" and "Issue" cards. Explore the picture and word sides of the card. Then remake your Best Picture adding in this new card's influence. This will create a revised picture that stands for a revised approach to dealing with your topic.

AN EXAMPLE OF CIRCUITS

For an example of the Circuits technique, let's look again at Ann's spread. In exploring the topic of her relationship with her daughter, Ann had received the Hole (#65) as the "You Now" and the Chair (#42) as "The Issue." These she located and marked on the Circle Pattern.

In Ann's case, there was only one simple and direct way to make a circuit; it was by the addition of #29, the Duck. Interestingly, that symbol had appeared in her spread in one of the "Behind You" positions.

When she had finished with the Best Picture from the Six-Step Process of Interpretation, Ann had a picture of a hole placed on a chair. She had interpreted this to mean integrating the inner and outer parts of herself, a unifying that would help her deal with her daughter. Adding the extra element of the Duck into the picture reintroduced a factor that had been part of the past of the topic.

AN EXAMPLE OF CIRCUITS

(In fact, the same symbol had come up for Ann in previous spreads on other topics about herself. Dealing with a recurring symbol, Ann found, can lead to greater insight.)

Ann reshaped the picture, creating this image: a chair sitting with its legs in a hole and a duck walking around the outside. The picture contained a great deal of meaning for Ann. The Duck was no longer a facade of levity that masked a more serious inner concern about the relationship. Now it represented the necessary cheeriness and naturalness that would help translate her own knowledge into actions that were more understandable to the daughter. She realized she had greeted the kind of self-expression the Duck represented with mixed emotions in the past. At times, she saw it as showing a cheerful acceptance, and at other times she saw it as indicating an avoidance of personal responsibility. The new picture brought the symbol into a more positive light. Also, combining the chair and hole indicated a more deliberate integration of her inner and outer aspects; they were more truly combined, yet each kept its own integrity. The chair was recognized, too, as being a very necessary aspect of structure, both for her own internal process as well as in guiding her daughter.

ANALYSIS BY STARS

Analysis by Stars is helpful in understanding the nature of any symbol. It is a way of using the Circle Pattern to identify the basic energy components that created the symbol. This analysis method can be especially beneficial when it has been difficult to see why a certain Symbolic Card occurred in a spread. The technique is explained for the "You Now" position, but it can be used with any symbol.

Since the yellow Star lines pass through all the numbered points on the Circle Pattern, each of those points can be seen as having been created by a certain mix of Star energies. Once a specific point is located on the circle, the basic energy ingredients for it are found by tracing back to the Star points that are directly connected to it.

These are the steps for Analysis by Stars:

1. On the Circle Pattern, mark the point that corresponds to the

number on your "You Now" card. (For lettered Star cards, an alternate method is given later.)

2. Find and mark the Star points that are connected to your point by straight yellow Star lines.

3. Find the corresponding Star cards and use the information on the word side of the cards to explore how these energies interact with each other. Stars close to your point have a stronger influence than those farther away. Stars equally distant from your point have an equal influence.

4. Reevaluate the idea of "You Now" in the Sky Spread in either of two ways: (a) in terms of how the different Star energies define and explain the "You Now" symbol; or (b) look at how each of the imaginary beings listed on the cards would deal with the symbol of "The Issue."

The goal is to get a better understanding of what energies comprise your "You Now" symbol, and to have a better idea of how it (and its ingredients) interacts with "The Issue."

EXAMPLE OF STAR ANALYSIS
In Ann's case, she looked at her "You Now" symbol plotted on the Circle Pattern, #65 Hole. She noted the yellow Star lines that passed through that point, and traced back along those lines to the Star points. The Star ingredients for the Hole were:

C. Star of Change: "The Mover"—*Adjusting*
E. Star of Laugh: "The Player"—*Externalizing*
H. Star of Hope: "The Prayer"—*Trusting*
L. Star of Patience: "The Dreamer"—*Imagining*

Stars C and E were equally close to, and Stars H and L were equally farther away from, her point.

Ann noted that the two closer energies (Adjusting and Externalizing) were both relatively active in nature. In contrast, the pair of energies farther away were rather passive. To her, this was a reflection of the quandary she had been in about internal and external parts of herself, and at the same time it was a very fair representation of the ability to combine those two facets, both a part of the Hole. Seeing the energies involved, she saw balance between the two more active energies and between the two more passive ones as well as a balance between the two pairs. Such balance was something she sought in herself and in her relationship with her daughter. She also noted that the slightly closer pair of energies were the more outgoing, and this helped her see that it was important to bring out of herself things that were developing within.

AN EXAMPLE OF ANALYSIS BY STARS

Ann also looked at how the imaginary beings from the cards would each deal with her symbol of "The Issue," the Chair. She saw "The Mover" as someone who would move the Chair, taking control in situations that arose in the relationship. "The Player" she saw as one who would use a chair as a stage prop, as a mime might use a simple prop to act out a variety of colorful roles. This indicated spontaneity in responding to issues with her daughter. Ann saw "The Prayer" as someone who would use the chair for praying, to gather insight. Similarly, "The Dreamer" rested on the chair, shaping the dreams that would become reality.

All in all, what Ann discovered through Analysis by Stars was the formula of basic energies at work within her symbol of the Hole. Although she uncovered few surprising new facts about the topic, it gave her a more organized way to understand impressions gathered earlier.

Since the symbol of the Duck had played such a key role in her spread, Ann chose also to look at the Star formula for it.

E. Star of Laugh: "The Player"—*Externalizing*
D. Star of Inwardness: "The Feeler"—*Internalizing*
G. Star of Indecision: "The Dancer"—*Weighing*
L. Star of Patience: "The Dreamer"—*Imagining*

The Duck is a Star-cross symbol. Star-crosses are the only points on the Circle Pattern where there is an unequal series of energies. Each Star is at a different distance from a Star-cross. Therefore, there is decidedly a leading energy whose influence prevails over all the others. In the case of all the other types of points (States, Gifts, and so on), there are pairs of co-equal energies. For the Duck, E is the closest star and L the farthest.

Ann saw within the symbol of the Duck that there were two very strong influences, the Stars of Laugh and Inwardness, and that the former was clearly the dominant influence, being the Star closest to her point. This meant that "The Player's" desire to externalize, to bring it all out, always won out over "The Feeler's" desire to take it all in. She found this very appropriate to the beneficial role this symbol had taken on for her, that it was necessary to act out inner awareness. She also noted that the energy of Weighing could add hesitancy and that again the energy of Imagining was involved, as it was in the Hole. She saw that there was a personal issue of dreams versus deeds, revealed by the repetition of active and passive energies in both symbols, the Hole and the Duck. But it was the key role of the Duck in revising her Best Picture (see pp. 179–80) that stressed the need to act more than think.

ALTERNATE METHOD (FOR STAR CARDS)

If the point in question is a Star point, it symbolizes a basic energy ingredient, not a mix of energies. Although the above method does not directly apply to Star points, you can learn more about a Star with the following method.

Find the lettered Star point on the Circle Pattern that corresponds to your Star card and mark it. This point will be one corner of a large square made by yellow Star lines. Find and mark the three Star points that make the other corners of the square.

The three other marked Stars play a role in relation to your Star. The energies of the two Stars that are on the corners of the large square *adjacent* to your Star can be seen as *supportive* of the energy of your Star. The energy of the Star *opposite* yours *opposes* the energy of your Star. Find the cards in the deck that correspond to these Star points. Use the cards' word side to discover which kinds of energy, moods, or atmospheres are helpful to you and which is a factor that limits or checks the energy of your own Star.

ANALYSIS BY HOUSES

Analysis by Houses gives you a way to compare where the "You Now" symbol is on the Circle Pattern versus where "The Issue" is. Although it is a qualitative analysis with much left to the interpretation of the player, it allows you to see where your position is on the Cycle of Growth about a specific topic. It also shows where your own growing edge is, by pinpointing where else on the cycle your attention is focused, where the issues are in terms of a topic.

In order to use this technique, you will need to be familiar with the idea of the Houses and the Garden structure as explained in the "Introduction to the Circle Pattern" (page 165).

Although the following explanation is written for the key cards in the Sky Spread, the "You Now" and "Issue," other symbols can be analyzed in the same manner.

These are the steps for Analysis by Houses:

1. Find and mark the two points on the Circle Pattern that correspond to your "You Now" and "Issue" cards.

2. Determine which Garden, and therefore which House, each point is in and mark those Houses near the outside of the Circle Pattern.

3. Remember: Both Stars and Gates are shared between two adjacent Houses. In the case of those points, mark both Houses they belong to.

4. Read the descriptions about the Houses you marked (see "Card Information," page 25). Compare how "The Issue" is in one House and the "You Now" in another. The House

descriptions should help restate or explain the nature of the topic.

5. Card Type or Level of Approach can also be taken into account, adding an important dimension to the analysis.

As an example of 4 and 5 above, suppose the Cup (#49) was your "You Now" card. Number 49 is located in House I on the Circle Pattern. The "You Now" has to do with one's basic self-expression; it pertains to the "I AM" part of the Cycle of Growth. Next, add in the fact that the Cup is a Key card, a challenge or realization. So "You Now," the Cup, represents the challenge of "I AM." With each card you analyze this way, try to complete the following sample sentences:

The "You Now" card is in the ___1st___ House, and so it relates to ___"I AM."___

"The Issue" card is in the _____ House, and so it relates to "I _____ ."

Then build on the sentences by adding in Card Type/Level of Approach; for example:

The "You Now" is a ___Key___ , and therefore it is the ___challenge___ of ___"I AM."___

"The Issue" is a ___(Card Type)___ , and therefore it is the ___(Level)___ of ___"I."___

Although this may seem awkward at first, learning to complete these sentences with the appropriate words will provide brief, meaningful statements about the Houses of your symbols. Below are some words related to Card Type/Level of Approach that will be of help in forming your own statements about the Houses.

TYPE	LEVEL	POSSIBLE WORDS
Star	Radiance	radiating, the light of, the energy of
State	Circumstance	the condition of, the state of
Star-cross	Expression	expressing, the expression of, acting out, demonstrating
Gift	Talent	the quality of, bringing out, the gift of

TYPE	LEVEL	POSSIBLE WORDS
Key	Challenge	the realization of, the challenge of, addressing, realizing
Gate	Attitude	the approach of, the gateway to, believing in
Sign	Fulfillment	the fulfillment of, the completion of, satisfying

EXAMPLE OF ANALYSIS BY HOUSES

When Ann did her analysis by Houses, she plotted her two main cards, the "You Now" and "Issue" (#65 Hole and #42 Chair), and saw, by looking at the Garden areas her points were in, that "The Issue" was related to the sixth House and her "You Now," being a Gate, was related to both the fourth and fifth Houses. The statements she formed read like this:

The "You Now" is in the ___4/5th___ Houses, and so it relates to both ___"I FEEL"___ and ___"I PROJECT."___

"The Issue" is in the ___6th___ House, and so it relates to ___"I BECOME."___

To Ann, exploring her relationship with her daughter, this aptly described the overall situation she was experiencing. She had felt both internal and external urges, typified by the fourth and fifth Houses, and she was trying to put it all together in order to be a better mother and friend to her daughter. When she added in Card Type/Level of Approach, her statements read like this:

The "You Now" is a ___Gate___ and therefore it is the ___approach___ of both ___"I FEEL"___ and ___"I PROJECT."___

"The Issue" is a ___Gift___, and therefore it is ___bringing out "I BECOME."___

To her, this was exactly the situation, but she had never seen it so clearly stated, in a way that was simple, true, and livable.

Ann also wanted to look at the House and Level of her extra card from the Circuits technique, #29 Duck. She found this was in the fifth House, and she made the following sentences:

AN EXAMPLE OF
ANALYSIS BY HOUSES

YOU NOW
"I PROJECT"

THE ISSUE
"I BECOME"

The Duck is in the ___5th___ House, and it relates to ___"I PROJECT."___

The Duck is a ___Star-cross___, and therefore it is the ___expression of "I PROJECT."___

To her, this was a message that she could really trust. It seemed right—for her, for her daughter, and for the relationship. The position of the Duck on the Circle Pattern looked almost like a bridge, a midway point, between where she had been and where she was headed, the key to getting from where she was to what she wanted.

ANALYSIS BY SEAS

This method is like Analysis by Houses in that it provides a rather qualitative feel for symbols. However, the Sea areas on the Circle Pattern are far more *subjective* in nature, whereas the Houses are more *objective*. Both Houses and Seas describe the universal Cycle of Growth, but the Seas speak more about the underlying qualities of growth than about their manifestations.

Also, only certain types of points occur in the Sea areas—Stars, Star-crosses, Keys, and Gates. The other types are not involved in terms of this analysis method because, with the Seas, the interior area is more significant than what lies along the borders.

The geography of the twelve Seas is explained in the "Introduction to the Circle Pattern" (page 165). However, the easiest way to spot the Seas is to look at the long tie-shaped *spaces* outlined in yellow Star lines lying between the Garden areas on the circle. Each of these is a Sea, with a Star point at its top, a Gate point at the base, and two Star-crosses and two Key points along the lines.

There are no actual steps required to perform this analysis. For any point you want to explore, such as the "You Now" or "Issue" symbols, mark the symbol on the Circle Pattern and determine the Sea it is in. Then read about that Sea (pages 205–218), and see what it adds to your understanding of the symbol. When plotting points in more than one Sea, you will notice relative differences in positions within the Cycle of Growth, just as you would with the Analysis by Houses technique.

EXAMPLE OF ANALYSIS BY SEAS

Ann looked at her "You Now" symbol, the Hole (#65), on the Circle Pattern and saw that it was a part of the fourth Sea, the Sea of Magic. Number 42, her "Issue" symbol, was outside a central Sea area, and so the method was not applicable to it. In reading about the Sea of Magic, Ann took note of her own inner wealth of strength and knowing. She realized that the Hole, a Gate to the area, indicated access to awareness and also provided a very needed outlet, a way to release her strength and vitality and put it to work.

Ann also wanted to know more about the symbol of the Duck, and she found that it was part of the next Sea in the cycle, the Sea of Laughing Hats (V). In reading about this area, she saw that the Duck was an expression of being in a role and enjoying it, of making the most of things regardless of the circumstances.

AN EXAMPLE OF
ANALYSIS BY SEAS

IV. SEA OF
MAGIC

V. SEA OF
LAUGHING HATS

THE
TWELVE
HOUSES

● ▲ ✚ ▼ ✖ ◪ ■

I

FIRST CAUSE

I. HOUSE OF THE FIRST CAUSE

"I AM"

This area has to do with one's basic self-expression, including likes and dislikes, disposition, and physical appearance.

The energies (Stars) of "I AM" are those of "The Dreamer" and "The Doer." The condition (State) is that of the Sand. The expressions (Star-crosses) are those of the Magician and the Wanderer. The Gift is in the Root, and the realization (Key) is through the Cup. The significant attitudes (Gates) are symbolized by the Tower and the Glove. Fulfillment (Sign) is the Mountain.

The Seas of Dreams and Time (XII and I) surround this Garden of "I AM."

II

MATRIX

II. HOUSE OF THE MATRIX

"I WANT"

The emphasis of this area is on resources at any level. These include pleasure, comfort, possessions, and wealth.

The energies (Stars) of the Matrix are those of "The Doer" and "The Speaker." The condition (State) is that of Lightning. The expressions (Star-crosses) are those of the Lover and the Tree. The Gift is the Eye. Realization (Key) is through the Rose. Significant attitudes (Gates) are symbolized by the Glove and the Ice. Fulfillment (Sign) is the Cake.

The Seas of Time and Innocence (I and II) surround this Garden of "I WANT.

III

MOTION

III. HOUSE OF THE MOTION

"I RELATE"

This area is concerned with comparing oneself to surroundings, with gathering information, and with communicating and socializing.

The energies (Stars) of the Motion are those of "The Speaker" and "The Mover." The condition (State) is that of Rain. The expressions (Star-crosses) are those of the Child and the Chest. The Gift is the Tunnel. The realization (Key) is through the Powder. Significant attitudes (Gates) are symbolized by the Ice and the Stone. Fulfillment (Sign) is the Cross.

The Seas of Innocence and Birth (II and III) surround this Garden of "I RELATE."

IV

PURE WATER

IV. HOUSE OF THE PURE WATER

"I FEEL"

This area has to do with satisfying inner needs, with feeling secure, and with one's emotions in general.

The energies (Stars) involved with the Pure Water are those of "The Mover" and "The Feeler." The condition (State) is that of Mud. The expressions (Star-crosses) are those of the Egg and the Glass. The Gift is the Harp, and realization (Key) is through the Serpent. Significant attitudes (Gates) are symbolized by the Stone and the Hole. Fulfillment (Sign) is the Sea.

The Seas of Birth and Magic (III and IV) surround this Garden of "I FEEL."

V

SPIRIT INCARNATE

V. HOUSE OF THE SPIRIT INCARNATE

"I PROJECT"

This area relates to how we express ourselves to others, our need to show creativity, and our need for validation and praise.

The energies (Stars) of the Spirit Incarnate are those of "The Feeler" and "The Player." The condition (State) is that of Fire. The expressions (Star-crosses) are those of the Moon and the Duck. The Gift is the Circle, and realization (Key) is through the Chain. Significant attitudes (Gates) are symbolized by the Hole and the Sword. Fulfillment (Sign) is the Star.

The Seas of Magic and Laughing Hats (IV and V) surround this Garden of "I PROJECT."

VI

GRAND PLAN

VI. HOUSE OF THE GRAND PLAN

"I BECOME"

This area concerns refining what we express, making use of our energy and the kinds of work or service we perform.

The energies (Stars) of the Grand Plan are those of "The Player" and "Majesty." The condition (State) is that of the Water. The expressions (Star-crosses) are those of the Jester and the Leaf. The Gift is in the Chair, and realization (Key) is through the Robe. Significant attitudes (Gates) are symbolized by the Sword and the Token. Fulfillment (Sign) is the Lamp.

The Seas of Laughing Hats and Kings (V and VI) surround this Garden of "I BECOME."

VII

PERFECT UNION

VII. HOUSE OF THE PERFECT UNION

"I INTERACT"

The emphasis here is on involvement with others, on relationships, partners, agreements, and all the ways we combine energies.

The energies (Stars) of the Perfect Union are those of "Majesty" and "The Dancer." The condition (State) is that of Earth. The expressions (Star-crosses) are those of the Maiden and the Bell. The Gift is the Letter, and realization (Key) is through the Gate. Significant attitudes (Gates) are symbolized by the Token and the Handle. Fulfillment (Sign) is the Cave.

The Seas of Kings and Music (VI and VII) surround this Garden of "I INTERACT."

VIII

POWER

VIII. HOUSE OF THE POWER

"I CARE"

This area represents the power that comes from combining with others, and learning the need for give and take—both within relationships and in oneself.

The energies (Stars) of the Power are those of "The Dancer" and "The Prayer." The condition (State) is that of Thunder. The expressions (Star-crosses) are those of the Butterfly and the Knife. The Gift is the Wheel, and realization (Key) is through the Wind. Significant attitudes (Gates) are symbolized by the Handle and the Rod. Fulfillment (Sign) is the Pearl.

The Seas of Music and Pyramids (VII and VIII) surround this Garden of "I CARE."

IX

ILLUMINATION

IX. HOUSE OF THE ILLUMINATION

"I REALIZE"

This area is concerned with the search for what is really true, for the basic principles in life, for what one truly believes in and values.

The energies (Stars) of the Illumination are those of "The Prayer" and "The Watcher." The condition (State) is that of Snow. The expressions (Star-crosses) are those of the Knight and the Ladder. The Gift is the Wing, and realization (Key) is through the Mask. Significant attitudes (Gates) are symbolized by the Rod and the Cherry. Fulfillment (Sign) is the Coffin.

The Seas of Pyramids and Labyrinths (VIII and IX) surround this Garden of "I REALIZE."

X

PERFECT FORM

X. HOUSE OF THE PERFECT FORM

"I PERFECT"

This area has to do with dealing with the truth, with confronting limitations and dealing with authority—both with others and within oneself.

The energies (Stars) of the Perfect Form are those of "The Watcher" and "The Deliverer." The condition (State) is that of Fog. The expressions (Star-crosses) are those of the Swan and the Window. The Gift is the Tongue, and realization (Key) is through the Block. Significant attitudes (Gates) are symbolized by the Cherry and the Arrow. Fulfillment (Sign) is the Field.

The Seas of Labyrinths and Quiet Flowers (IX and X) surround this Garden of "I PERFECT."

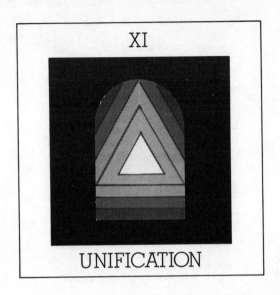

XI

UNIFICATION

XI. HOUSE OF THE UNIFICATION

"I EXPAND"

The emphasis here is on one's highest hopes, to surpass limitation and reach for freedom—not just for oneself but for all.

The energies (Stars) of the Unification are those of "The Deliverer" and "The Seeker." The condition (State) is that of Air. The expressions (Star-crosses) are those of the Sun and the Fountain. The Gift is the Morning, and realization (Key) is through the Wand. Significant attitudes (Gates) are symbolized by the Arrow and the Siphon. Fulfillment (Sign) is the Crown.

The Seas of Quiet Flowers and Stars Within (X and XI) surround this Garden of "I EXPAND."

XII

DISSOLUTION

XII. HOUSE OF THE DISSOLUTION

"I MERGE"

This area represents achieving fulfillment and, through absolute completion, transcending and dissolving back into the Whole.

The energies (Stars) of the Dissolution are those of "The Seeker" and "The Dreamer." The condition (State) is that of the Pool. The expressions (Star-crosses) are those of the Monk and the Candle. The Gift is the Rope, and realization (Key) is through the Ring. Significant attitudes (Gates) are symbolized by the Siphon and the Tower. Fulfillment (Sign) is the Key.

The Seas of Stars Within and Dreams (XI and XII) surround this Garden of "I MERGE."

THE
TWELVE
SEAS

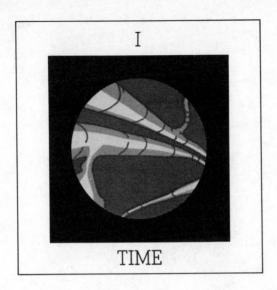

I

TIME

I. SEA OF TIME

EXPERIENCING

In this Sea we exist and experience. Duration leads to sequence, and we separate then from now, this from that, and you from me. Everybody wants to do something; we stir.

Here shines the Star of Impulse, "The Doer." He fills this place with the desire to experience. The expressions (Star-crosses) are the Wanderer and the Lover. The realizations (Keys) are in the Cup and the Rose. The way in and out is through the Gate of the Glove, where PROJECTING IDENTITIES gains access and AC-CEPTING ASSISTANCE creates an exit.

The Sea of Time is shared between the first and second Houses, the First Cause and the Matrix.

II

INNOCENCE

II. SEA OF INNOCENCE

GROWING

In this place we still hear the voice of "The Speaker," that which sent us forth and beckons us onward. Under the Star of Reaching, we GROW and pursue living.

The expressions (Star-crosses) are the Child and the Tree. The realizations (Keys) are through the Rose and the Powder. Access and exit are through the Gate of the Ice, where CLARITY gets one in and CHANGEABILITY lets one out. Here we recall our inner guidance.

The Sea of Innocence is shared between the second and third Houses, the Matrix and the Motion.

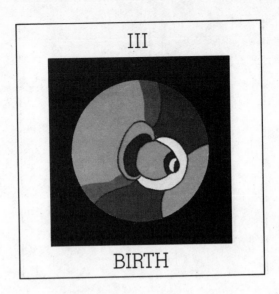

III

BIRTH

III. SEA OF BIRTH

ADJUSTING

In this Sea the Star of Change brings forth new things. "The Mover" acts; the energy of ADJUSTING makes way for new emergence. This is the East, where dawn brings opportunity.

The expressions (Star-crosses) are the Egg and the Chest. The realizations (Keys) are in the Powder and the Serpent. The Gate is the Stone, providing entry through INTEGRITY and exit through STEADFASTNESS.

The Sea of Birth is shared between the third and fourth Houses, the Motion and the Pure Water.

IV

MAGIC

IV. SEA OF MAGIC

INTERNALIZING

Here the Mystery comes forth, just beneath the fabric of life, a buoyant undercoat woven by "The Feeler." Through the energy of INTERNALIZING, that which is latent congeals. We are not powerless and simply placed on Earth; we feel the wonder within.

The expressions (Star-crosses) are the Moon and the Glass. The realizations (Keys) are in the Serpent and the Chain. The Gate of the Hole provides access through PERCEPTION OF OTHER REALITIES and exit through OPENNESS.

The Sea of Magic is shared between the fourth and fifth Houses, the Pure Water and the Spirit Incarnate.

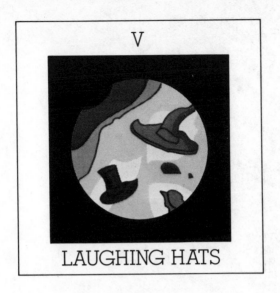

V

LAUGHING HATS

V. SEA OF LAUGHING HATS

EXTERNALIZING

In this Sea are all life's actors, each with permission to act out his or her role. "The Player" eggs us on. He encourages us to enjoy being onstage with his energy of EXTERNALIZING. We can be anything we choose, at least for a moment.

The expressions (Star-crosses) are the Jester and the Duck. The realizations (Keys) are through the Chain and the Robe. Entry and exit are through the Gate of the Sword, where SELF-EXPRESSION makes a way in and DISCRIMINATING creates the way out.

The Sea of Laughing Hats is shared between the fifth and sixth Houses, the Spirit Incarnate and the Grand Plan.

VI

KINGS

VI. SEA OF KINGS

INTEGRATING

In the southerly position, "Majesty," the Star of Bowing, reigns. The energy of INTEGRATING calls forth our best, seeking a blend of inner and outer urges and exposure of our transcendent nature. We glimpse our personal glory and our collective heritage.

The expressions (Star-crosses) are the Leaf and the Maiden. The realizations (Keys) are through the Robe and the Gate. The Gate to Kings is through the Token, where entry comes from AP-PRECIATING OTHERS and exit from EXPRESSING INTENT.

The Sea of Kings is shared between the sixth and seventh Houses, the Grand Plan and the Perfect Union.

VII

MUSIC

VII. SEA OF MUSIC

WEIGHING

In this place we experience "The Dancer," the vibration of life between polarities. We feel the pulsating current of existence and know the balance of things through the energy of WEIGHING.

The expressions (Star-crosses) are the Bell and the Butterfly. The realizations (Keys) are in the Gate and the Wind. Entry and exit are provided by the Gate of the Handle, a paradoxical mix of INITIATIVE and RESPONSIBILITY.

The Sea of Music is shared between the seventh and eighth Houses, the Perfect Union and the Power.

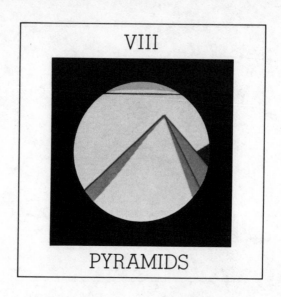

VIII

PYRAMIDS

VIII. SEA OF PYRAMIDS

TRUSTING

In this Sea we discover the heights to which we can aspire and, equally, the depths to which we can tumble. Here the Star of Hope shines ardently; "The Prayer" communes most sincerely. But his cause is serious and deep; self-righteousness is a temptation. One must examine the motives for great deeds, or fall.

The expressions (Star-crosses) are the Knight and the Knife. The realizations (Keys) are in the Wind and the Mask. The Gate to Pyramids is through the Rod, where COMMAND provides entry and DISCRETION makes an exit.

The Sea of Pyramids is shared between the eighth and ninth Houses, the Power and the Illumination.

IX

LABYRINTHS

IX. SEA OF LABYRINTHS

PERCEIVING

In this place we view the complexities of life along with the seeming ultimate arbitrariness of it all. This is the West, where the Star of Austerity perplexes us with the steady gaze of "The Watcher." The energy of PERCEIVING is intense, unblinking. It is the puzzle of puzzles, the challenge of silence, the unuttered question with no conceivable answer. It is the place of the most final of questions.

The expressions (Star-crosses) are the Swan and the Ladder. The realizations (Keys) are in the Mask and the Block. The Gate is the Cherry, where GETTING INVOLVED creates access and INNER COMPLETION makes the way out.

The Sea of Labyrinths is shared between the ninth and tenth Houses, the Illumination and the Perfect Form.

X

QUIET FLOWERS

X. SEA OF QUIET FLOWERS

FREEING

Over this Sea shines the Star of Independence. The light of "The Deliverer" urges us to set ourselves free. Together we create a field of beauty with its own reason and purpose. Free yet together—that is this place.

The expressions (Star-crosses) are the Sun and the Window. The realizations (Keys) are in the Block and the Wand. The Gate is the Arrow, where SPONTANEITY creates a way in and DECISIVENESS makes the way out.

The Sea of Quiet Flowers is shared between the tenth and eleventh Houses, the Perfect Form and the Unification.

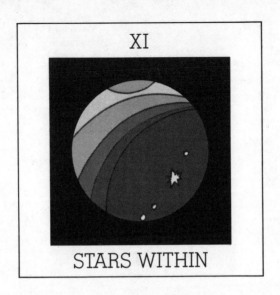

XI

STARS WITHIN

XI. SEA OF STARS WITHIN

DISCOVERING

Here we experience our own transcendence. The Star of Aspiration shines, and "The Seeker" is revealed to himself through the transparent energy of DISCOVERING. We find we are god-stuff and star-stuff. We see through ourselves to the truth; we were never apart. We become both mind and energy, Star and Gate as one.

The expressions (Star-crosses) are the Monk and the Fountain. The realizations (Keys) are in the Wand and the Ring. The Gate is the Siphon, where EXCHANGE is the way in and RELEASE is the way out.

The Sea of Stars Within is shared between the eleventh and twelfth Houses, the Unification and the Dissolution.

XII

DREAMS

XII. SEA OF DREAMS

IMAGINING

In this place one experiences the beginning and ending of things—
the spark, the idea. It is the North, the unknowable, the Mystery.
It is where all things come from, the unlimited potential of "The
Dreamer." We swirl in all that can be, before and after it is real.

The expressions (Star-crosses) are the Magician and the Candle.
The realizations (Keys) are in the Ring and the Cup. The Gate is
the Tower, where REFLECTION provides access and FOCUSING
ATTENTION makes a way out.

The Sea of Dreams is shared between the twelfth and first
Houses, the Dissolution and the First Cause.

AFTERWORD- THE STORY BEHIND STAR+GATE

● ▲ ✦ ▼ ✕ ◣ ■

From the center of nothingness, from silence, came the voice:

"Hear me,
I am inside you.
Behold what I am
and never be afraid again,
nor ever fear
one thing in thy world.

"I am the seed that has grown you.
You need never fear,
for I am with you,
always,
forever.

"I am the Wings of Heaven,
the Bosom of Love,
the Herald of Truth everlasting.
Yet you cannot see me,
so deep am I within you,
so far spread am I without,
through the multitude,
throughout the universe,
I live throughout all things.

"All lives within my dream,
my eyes, my wonder,
my caring and my loose stroke.
all that has been named,
all that can be known,
all dwells within my silence,
all dwells within my glorious expanse.

"Know always that I am with you.
You shall never
be
alone."

WHERE DID STAR+GATE COME FROM?

In the classic story by Frank Baum, the Tin Man found he had a heart, the Scarecrow brains, the Lion courage, and Dorothy her way home. Their realizations came from adventures that revolved around the Wizard of Oz in the Emerald City.

Following the yellow brick road and arriving at the center of the kingdom, Dorothy and her friends received an audience with the mysterious, awe-inspiring wizard. Later they discovered the maker of all the magic, the man behind the curtain. He was, after all, simply a man seated at a keyboard that produced the magnificent sounds of bells and whistles, a man whose heart was indeed touched by the plight of Dorothy—for he, too, had once been a stranger in the land of Oz.

As the person behind STAR+GATE, I am pulling the curtains aside to say something about myself and how this work came about. STAR+GATE represents a realization of my own, which occurred nearly twenty years ago. I didn't plan it, nor did I have credentials for getting into this type of work.

What has happened to me is not very startling, not the result of alien visitors, channeled spirits, or seeing holy men. Yet I had experiences that were profound for me, and I believed they would lead to a clearer understanding of life.

While a college student majoring in art, a talent that came naturally to me, questions and wonderings from earlier years began to

223

come to a head. Although an artistic career was natural to pursue, it somehow left me unsatisfied. What I wanted to know was: Why am I here? What is life all about? What am I supposed to be doing? More important to me than school were countless long conversations with friends about the nature of people, the world, life, and God. We pushed ourselves to deepen our understanding of the universe.

Then, in my third year of college, I took a course in architecture to complete my major. At first it seemed nothing more than a survey of old buildings and monuments. Gradually, though, I started realizing something new about life. Through architecture I began to see the sincerity of man's struggle for meaning and understanding. Art, for me, had always emphasized the artist's vision, one person's expression. Architecture seemed to point to a history-long quest for meaning and purpose. It began to dawn on me that I was like many, many others in the world who faced the same questions and issues. In some way I was like every man, and every man was like me. If I was lost, so were many others. What had seemed like a purposeless life—starting nowhere, aiming nowhere, and getting nowhere—suddenly had meaning. In my own way, I was striving for meaning and understanding, and so was everyone else, each in an individual way, each with his or her own abilities and hang-ups.

One day, as I was walking through a doorway into a sunny afternoon, the world and time seemed to stop completely. In that one instant everything made *perfect sense.* In that moment I realized that everything I had seen or done or had experienced—all of it—had been *perfectly* planned, choreographed, and staged for me for my own growth. I had always had a choice in what happened, and yet every bit of my life had been for my benefit. A marvelous feeling of insight, of really "getting the point" about things, came over me. I felt a grand sense of cooperation, whether I had been conscious of it or not, between the world at large and myself. Imagine! Each event, each experience, tailored just for me! And the same exquisite arrangement existed for everyone else, regardless of whether they knew it or not.

I wish it hadn't taken almost twenty years to glimpse the truth, beauty, and magic of living, to put aside questioning and discover my own becoming. Seeing the sense of it all, confusion faded and was replaced by a goal: to help project and explain this feeling of

224

"place" in the world, in space, and in time. I felt everyone deserved to experience this understanding and participation with their lives that I had been able to realize for myself. Seeing that the design of life is fluid, that we help shape it and within it we are shaped, is to be in step with things.

COULD THE UNIVERSE BE AS SIMPLE AS A CHILD'S GAME?

My realization of purpose in life reduced my anxiety. If I was lost, eventually I would be found. Life, and being in it, was still a great mystery, but I now felt challenged to solve it.

I started looking for ways to express man's quest—games, models, systems, patterns that had to do with meaning. Each exploration, each creation, took me closer to an idea, that within the game of life there might be found, or created, a game that revealed the nature of life. The idea of hunting for a game about The Game made more sense the more I thought about it. It satisfied my longing for an explanation or map to help me through life.

I examined some of the games and systems of thought that already existed. I was aware of Tarot and had tried it a few times. I was fascinated by it, but after a few experiences with it I decided it wasn't for me. I had similar feelings about I Ching. I knew it was a good system, but it didn't satisfy me. And so it was with other systems I encountered. None had the quality I was after. This brief review, however, made me realize I had a feeling for what I was seeking, and that feeling was *acting as a guide.* Perhaps I could peer into that feeling, make it larger and clearer, make it unfold and help reveal the goal—an underlying pattern.

The time was the late sixties, and all across the country people were asking questions. They were aware of more than one simple, black-and-white reality in life. Each different state opened a different yet somehow valid perspective on life. I remember thinking: What's the reality of all these realities? What do they have in common? Is there a pattern, a model they are all based on?

Dozing one afternoon, I saw an image in my mind that put things into a context. I saw a circle with myself standing within it, but I was in several places at once. The circle itself looked like a phonograph record, with some concentric rings and other lines, and near the center was a deep, round void. Half dreaming, I realized that the different places where I saw myself standing could represent different states of mind. Each state of mind was just a different place from which to view the rest of the circle. And from any spot within the circle, I could turn and see all of the circle. This image made a simple kind of sense. A feeling of something profound stirred deep within me.

If what I saw in my mind's eye actually applied to how things worked in life, then this could be a very important discovery. I reasoned that if this image was a reflection of life, the whole of life must be visible from any vantage point, including mine. Perhaps, then, there were no secrets in the universe, just self-imposed blinders and veils. I also reasoned that what I could see in my mind's eye was just another perspective, a method of gaining insight into the everyday world. The inner world and outer or physical world, I reasoned, must be alike in some fashion—one a reflection of the other. To me, that meant some real model or game must exist in the physical world—just as the mental image existed inside of me—that could reveal truths about life.

Where to begin looking for such a model in the everyday world, I had no idea. I decided to have faith, to trust the way things were working, and to remain open and receptive. It was only a few days later that I found my model in a full-page ad for a book on astrology. The ad, on the back page of the comics section of the Sunday newspaper, showed several of the book's diagrams and illustrations. One diagram was a circle with a series of overlapping triangles that connected the Fire, Earth, Air, and Water signs of the zodiac. Where the triangles crossed over one another, I saw Water crossing Earth, Fire crossing Water, and so on.

All at once I realized that the essentials and dynamics of life could be as simple as the child's game of Rock, Paper, and Scissors. This revelation was like seeing a universal chemistry or alchemy occurring before me, based on a simple diagram of natural elements. It dawned on me that, based on what I was seeing, a table of elements could be set up that would convey the essences of life and their ways of interrelating—a table of life that was simple yet complex, like life itself. And although this table would be comprised of elements of the everyday world, like fire and water and so on, it would describe the deep expansive levels of awareness that existence also contains.

It is difficult to convey all the thoughts, impressions, and feelings that ran through me in those brief moments of realization. It was a flashing glimpse of what such a system could be, what it could reveal, and what it could do for people. I sensed there was an enormous amount of information there for the asking, for anyone who wanted to know. And here I was, the first in line. I was thrilled; it was like finding the Grail at the bottom of the clothes hamper.

The problem was, though, that I hadn't the slightest notion of what to do with the diagram and all these ideas. I had wanted something like this, believed in the idea, and then found it right under my nose, right here in the physical world. So physical reality wasn't shallow or incomplete after all. Within it were many rich and meaningful things. I could work with it, not feel apart from it. And what had gotten me to this point was trusting in my own feelings, using a hunch or intuition as a guide. This meant that by using both the rational and intuitive parts of myself I could discover more than I could with either part alone. I felt all the parts of me coming together, each with its own role. I was ready to go on the journey, not knowing where it would lead. All I knew was that it felt right, and that would be my guide.

I began that very day working with some drafting equipment. I re-created the diagram from the newspaper and started playing around with it. I was interested in the intersecting triangles—for example, where the line from the Fire triangle crossed the one from Water. The sketch that caught my attention was a series of lines that paralleled the lines of the four triangles. As I looked at it, I saw it spin, whirl within itself, unfold yet lead back into itself. I saw it do many things, and it seemed to express much and explain much. It was only a pencil drawing on a piece of plain yellow paper, but from deep within I knew I had found what I was looking for.

I mused over the pencil diagram off and on for the rest of the day. Ideas and plans swam around in my head and became a part of my dreams that night. In the morning I bought art supplies to fashion a game board—thin, colored tapes; round, stick-on dots; and a nice piece of redwood board.

I translated the sketch onto the game board by what was becoming standard operating procedure: working by intuition. First were the lines that seemed to call for blue tape. These lines swept across the circle dividing it into parts from edge to edge. Next were a group of lines that seemed to call for green. These lines were like a web and appeared to add a sense of structure to the pattern. Those lines that were left I made in yellow. These seemed to light up the circle, making it appear vibrant and alive. Together, all three colors made a pattern that was pleasing, active, and soothing at the same time. Next, I chose round yellow dots to mark certain intersections within the pattern, places that seemed more important to my eye than others. There were 108 spots when I had marked them all.

The Circle Pattern was complete. I could tell by the way it looked, and I was amazed at what I saw. My feeling was like that of a child who stands back for a moment from his scratching and digging in the sand to discover he has built a castle. It seemed a majestic thing.

There was much to learn from the Circle Pattern, and I spent the next three months almost completely engrossed with it. I wanted to know for myself all it could reveal about life. There it lay before me, silently inviting me to know it. I had only the barest of guidelines, the original connection with astrology, and the sense of intuition that had brought me this far in my search.

First, I explored the lines. I named the blue ones Cloud lines. Why? Because it felt right, and I trusted that sooner or later I would discover there was a reason for them being called by that name. The twelve areas these lines described I named the Houses, and where they merged toward the circle's center was a thirteenth area, which I called the Hall of Signs.

Looking at the green lines, I saw two kinds. There were the ones that ran from close to the circle's edge right to the center of the pattern. These seemed, in some way, to contain the essence of each House area; they ran right through each House's center, joining at the pattern's center. I called these Lineage lines. The other type of green lines spanned the circle's perimeter, linking the Lineage lines through what seemed like the arm-in-arm embrace of a ring of brothers and sisters around the circle. These I named Bridges.

Where the Bridges crossed one another was where the yellow lines emanated. Yellow lines paralleled the angles of both the blue and green lines, but they seemed to do so at a different level. Because they were bright yellow, I decided to call them Star lines. I chose also to name the points of their emanation Star points.

Except for one ring of twelve points, which was the outermost ring on the circle, all of the other points I had marked on the circle fell within the ring of Star points. In fact, they were all on the intersections of yellow Star lines. It looked as though each of the points in a way contained the emanations of the Stars whose lines met at this or that point. It dawned on me that I was beginning to see the fruits of my intuition; there was a method before me for checking my work. And this merits some explanation.

Developing the game, especially at this early stage, was not a simple linear progression of ideas. Instead, it seemed ideas and impressions were going off like firecrackers in every direction in my head, many at the same time. I held each possibility as valid until it panned out or reached a dead end. Each tentative development affected all the previous choices and those to follow. But gradually the terminology and geography of STAR+GATE came together, like pieces of a puzzle. However, it seemed that several lines of thought were always present, steeping in my mind.

Early on, I got the impression there would be two main parts of the game. The Circle Pattern map I was exploring was one, and the other would be symbols related to the map. Working from my original theory that each reality and each viewpoint in a reality contains a vision of the whole, I felt that the objects in our every-day world could be used as simple evocative symbols to describe essences—just as in Rock, Paper, and Scissors—from beneath the atoms to beyond the gods. And, as I worked with the Circle Pattern, as I have described, I was also thinking about the set of symbols—their names, their positions within the circular pattern, and what form these should take to complete the game.

As these ideas congealed, there grew out of the process a method for checking the intuitive work. The entire system might turn out to be insanity or the most accurate thing ever conceived, but it had to make sense within its own context; the system had to be rational, too. So, for instance, if I decided that my "gut feeling" said black would be the color for one spot, the spot exactly opposite it had better be white or there should be a good reason why it was not.

As it turned out, the connection the circle had with astrology and the web of lines and points within the Stars gave me a context for evaluating my work. From a book on astrology I chose the names of the twelve Houses on the circle based on the signs of the

229

zodiac. And from a distillation of several astrological facets, I named the Star points. The former group divided the circle into areas that related to the development of personality and self. The latter described the essential energies or types of activity that beings exhibit. By that time I also had a list of simple everyday things (a robe, a chest, a maiden, and so on) that I felt most people would recognize and were rich in symbolism, full of possible meanings. I went through the list, seeing where each symbol might belong on the circle.

Now there were criteria to help check intuitive impressions. When I thought a symbol name belonged in a particular place, I would also check whether it made sense within the system. I questioned whether the name of the symbol met the criteria that were developing, how the point got that name, and then I went on to another symbol. The process was a slow one.

As the points were named, I created a simple set of cards (pencil drawings on card stock) to capture the images I had in mind for each. There were ninety-six cards when I finished, plus twelve more to represent the House areas.

My original discovery of the model was in August 1968; by early November I had achieved a complete and usable game. There were now two game boards side by side, one for the Circle Pattern and the other for laying out the cards. I worked out a method for playing the game that went something like this: With a specific topic in mind, I looked at the twelve House cards that were placed around the outside of the Circle. Depending on the nature of the topic, I would select the appropriate House. From that area of the circle, I entered the pattern, placing a wooden marker on a Star point and then moving through the rest of the circle with markers and dice. As I landed on each spot, I drew the corresponding numbered card from the deck and placed it in a relative position on the blank game board. When I was finished moving, I had two boards to interpret for insights into my topic—the markers placed on relative spots on the Circle Pattern and the cards arranged on the other board.

Each time I used it, I was amazed at what I saw. The symbols I received triggered vivid and touching insights about real situations I was dealing with. The feeling was like being at the control board of one's life, a vantage point for seeing things from a clear and true perspective. I didn't receive any pat answers to my questions; the system wasn't set up to do that. What I got instead, through the imagery of symbols, was real perspective, and with that at hand, I could easily see how best to proceed with issues in my life.

At first a hazy concept, my "game" was now a useful and revealing tool. I felt the next step was to share this unusual tool with others.

FIRST PLAYER

Laura—a friend whose kitchen table was the hub of music, art, and the counterculture in the small town where I attended college— was the first person to try out my creation. I knew that if she liked the game, her friends far and wide would hear about it.

As she looked at the large geometric design on the table, at the piles of markers and dice, and at the stack of cards, it was obvious she thought she was in over her head. I told her not to worry; I would show her how to do everything. All she had to do was play along.

"Just think of something you want to know about," I said.

"I can't really think of anything, I mean, unless it's the whole thing."

"The whole thing?" I asked. "You mean your *life?*"

"Yeah, that's what I want to do, look at my whole life. Can we do that? Is that okay?"

"Well, sure, if it's okay with you, Laura," I said.

Off we went. I showed her how to move the dice and markers and where to place the cards. In a few minutes, moving on the circle was finished, and she had an array of cards laid out in front of her. She sat there in silence, looking at the cards as though they were hieroglyphics.

"I don't think I get it," she said. "What's it supposed to mean?"

"I don't know, Laura; whatever it means to you. All I know is you wanted to look at your life, and there it is—that's it."

She sat and looked at the cards some more. I worried that she was just being polite, doing me a favor. I began to feel uncomfortable. Maybe this game was strictly for me. Maybe I should have tried it on someone else. Maybe I was expecting too much, of the game and of Laura.

Then, as I was about to call the whole thing off, her eyes got huge and her mouth dropped open. "Oh, my God. It's all . . . right . . . there!"

She saw her entire life spread before her, her truth. Thanks to Laura, I knew right then that I wasn't the only one this system worked for.

Thus began an endless string of evenings, sometimes at Laura's kitchen table, sometimes at my own place. People wanted to see the game, to see for themselves why so-and-so had had such an indescribable experience. There was hardly a night that two or three or more people weren't with me, discovering themselves and the game. This went on from November through the following spring. During this time, I'm sure, a type of aura grew up around the game and myself, ranging from eerie to mystical. People came who were so primed by their friends that they were spooked just walking through the door. Others came to check me out. But mostly, they came to have a special experience, and that's what any willing player got, a special insight into him or her self.

After graduation from college I moved in with a friend who introduced me to the woman I married soon after, and I got a job. These circumstances caused me to put marketing the game on hold for several years.

I continued to work on the game, learning more about it and developing it. I used it for my own guidance and shared it with others, but not as intensely as before. I experimented with many styles and sizes of cards, with new formats and spread arrangements, but it was mainly a hobby.

ENTER THE PSYCHICS

About four years later, in 1974, I started meeting people involved in psychic phenomena and self-exploration. The game blossomed in that atmosphere. Anything about it that was esoteric or hard to describe made it all the more appealing.

All this led to another key development in the game. These people, whether they were the teachers or the students, expected a psychic reading from me and my game. Most were accustomed to having a psychic or some authority tell them what was going on or even tell them what to do. When they looked to me for that kind of information, I just looked back at them. They would stare at the cards they received, but not trust their own vision to lead them to the answers. On occasion, I tried to help them with interpretation. But just as often, I got angry at myself for getting sucked into the role of expert. Then I'd say, "Look, what you see in the cards is more important than what I see. After all, you know more about your own life and your own truth than I ever could. Get in touch with yourself."

Well, some did and some didn't. I didn't know how to handle these situations, but in reaction I started working on what has become a key part of the game—words. Some people had a hard time making mental associations with pictures. That was all the cards contained at that time, just a name and a picture on one side and nothing on the other. When I suggested related words to people who were stuck, suddenly they discovered meaningful associations. I decided that if I could give a player a list of words for the cards, the task of interpretation might be a lot easier. And with use of the words, the responsibility for interpretation would fall back on the player, where it rightfully belonged.

I sought out several of my friends for help. I deliberately asked different types of people, seeking a variety of ideas and opinions. In all, seven of us embarked on the project: to make a list of seven or eight key words for each of the ninety-six cards. I thought it would take a few weekends. Fourteen months later, after countless sessions that I called controlled arguments, with battered notebooks and frayed pages with doodles, erasures, and cross-outs, we finally completed our list of words.

Typed and contained in a thin notebook, the list became an integral part of the game. The game now provided the player with both verbal and visual information. Generally, the new game was a more rewarding experience for more people, and my role was reduced to showing the game, not interpreting it.

GETTING PUSHED OVER THE EDGE AGAIN

By now it was 1978, a year that turned out to be full of surprises. It started out innocently enough, with a trip to the movies on New Year's Day.

Recovering from celebrating the new year, my wife and I decided to go see the new movie *Close Encounters of the Third Kind.* The film reminded me poignantly of my own life, of believing in something and not having the words to convey it, of struggling to materialize an idea even at the expense of appearing the fool, of sensing the approach of something glorious, of having a role in it but never knowing exactly the what, where, or why of it all.

Soon after came a surprise. Two months into the year I was fired from my job. In a major office reorganization, several positions were eliminated. My boss tried to be kind, but in a matter of weeks I was to be out.

Getting fired was a jolt, like getting hit right between the eyes. But I knew it was a message. It was "fish or cut bait." It was time to act on my hidden desires or forget them. If I didn't do something about the game now, I never would. I was scared, and I felt cornered. And yet I felt freed from what I had been doing and challenged to take on what I always said I cared about: the game and what it could do for people.

After a great deal of talking to myself, talking with my wife, and talking with friends, I made a decision. One way or another, this was my opportunity to produce the game. If I failed, at least I had tried.

Now it was time to really plan, to find out what the project would take, to know what we had and what we needed. I called together several friends to talk the whole thing out. Out of a long evening's pow-wow, it became clear that among us we had many of the talents and resources needed to produce the game.

Out of that meeting grew a team who would launch the game, one way or another. The following nine months were spent preparing the launch, from product development to testing to packaging to financing the endeavor. Most of the key people involved gave freely of their time, knowing that one day they would be compensated and that one day, because of their efforts, the game would be out in the world. These people gave me tremendous support at a time when I had chosen to proceed on faith. Knowing how risky such a project would be, though, I worked as thoroughly and carefully as possible to avoid the traditional mistakes and natural pitfalls that accompany any kind of self-publishing.

The development that occurred on the game during those

months was significant in making it what it is today. After testing the game on consumers, we found the format far too complicated. I was forced to consider breaking the game into two parts, to sell the cards on their own and release Circle Pattern as a separate item later. At the time, it seemed ridiculous to reduce all that went into the game down to a set of cards, and yet it had to be done to make it more accessible.

In thinking it through, I realized the word list could be incorporated into the cards by printing the words on the cards' backs. At first it seemed like an awkward approach, yet the idea fit. We observed that some people were more at home with pictures, others were more at ease with words.

As we tried a prototype deck on the team, a process of interpretation began to develop, a process of turning cards from one side to the other in an organized procedure.

Despite my reservations, the changes and refinements were making the game easier to understand and use. From our makeshift consumer testing, we observed people coming away from playing the game not only liking it but liking themselves better, too. We were finding acceptance—even from people who didn't go for "that kind of thing."

TELL ME YOUR NAME

During this period of final development, I went around in circles mentally, trying to find the right name for the game. Such an unusual game or system or method—whatever it was—seemed to defy description with the usual kind of name. Yet trust and intuition had gotten me this far, not knowing had led to knowing, so I believed the right name would come in its own time.

Then one day, driving on the freeway, it occurred to me to let the thing name itself. Star and Gate cards were two of the most significant kinds of cards in the deck. Stars represent basic types of activity, and Gates represent mind. Stars and Gates, in the language of the game, succinctly described the human condition— energy of life channeled through the postures of the mind. The terms also described for me a broader idea, that of spirit weaving through form. Stars with Gates equaled people. Stars plus Gates also equaled a universe. It was like an equation: STAR + GATE.

THE LARGER DREAM

Where did STAR+GATE come from? What is its purpose? I have often been asked these questions by people who have experienced the system. My answers probably haven't been all that satisfying, for I have no clear and simple answers. I know that STAR+GATE is not new, not something I invented. On the other hand, it is not from antiquity, not rediscovered. I have said at different times that STAR+GATE came from the Sunday funnies and from the search of a befuddled artist. Both are true in a way, but I know that the system was not thought up, by me or anyone beyond me.

STAR+GATE is, I believe, timeless or beyond time as we know it. There is a freshness about the pattern and all that flows from it, but that speaks more of what is to come than of anything else. STAR+GATE, which began as a unique "game" and evolved into a system for intuition and creativity, is a gift, and I know now that, in part, I came to deliver the gift. The questions of where it came from and what its purpose is have been with me since I first discovered the Circle Pattern, the deepest expression of the system. Having spent so many years with it, I have plenty of thoughts about it. But its meaning and use are not up to me; they are up to you, the thousands of people around the world who use it, and the new users still to come. You and they will ultimately be the ones to decide what is to become of it.

I have been delighted and sometimes astonished at the coincidences involving STAR+GATE that have cropped up. In literature, art, and other areas of expression, it appears that similar ideas have been on many minds. Those ideas may point to a long-range future for STAR+GATE that is only beginning to emerge. Here are some examples of what I mean:

○ Just after the basic game was created, I discovered a lesser-known work of Hermann Hesse, *Magister Ludi* subtitled *The Glass Bead Game.* It tells of a culture in which the ruling class are full-time players of a sophisticated game of meaning. On a patterned matrix players place and move colored beads. The meanings associated with the activity are such that a poet and a mathematician could play together, for example, one expressing a subtle nuance of poetic expression and the other understanding the same configuration in terms of an elegant mathematical equation. It was a sort of language of languages where many disciplines could be expressed and understood. The simple yet classical set of STAR+GATE symbols, contained within the matrix of the Circle Pattern, presents the same potential.

○ Roger Zelazney, a noted science-fiction writer, produced a series of books on the theme of Amber, a place from which Earth and all other realms stemmed. Amber contained a "pattern" that depicted the cosmos. The pattern contained seven veils of energy, each more difficult to penetrate than the last. Only the Princes of Amber could walk the pattern at all, and he who could, commanded the forces of the universe as well as being able to appear at other replicas of the pattern found in other realms. Also, each Prince had a set of symbolic cards, which included trumps—portrait cards of the Princes and other members of Amber's Court. By looking intensely at a certain trump, a Prince would gain instant communication with the person pictured; staring harder would teleport him to wherever the person actually was.

○ *The Game Players of Zan,* by M. A. Foster, tells of a mutant race of humans living side by side with their counterparts on Earth. They were an experiment that apparently was a dud, producing a simple, agrarian people distinguished only by an odd fascination with a stylized game played by two ruling families. It turns out that their life-style is a cover for a powerful game that involves juggling the very forces of nature. The player families, one discovers, have actually been bred as pilots for an evolving interspace vehicle housed in a mountain. The spaceship is so advanced that it has a consciousness of its own which, when evolved enough, will blast away from Earth bearing the new race, their pilots at its helm. Through the delicate interplay of cosmic forces embodied in their "game," the pilots learn how to guide and steer the ship.

○ C. G. Jung had on the wall in his bedroom a mandala he used for meditation that had been specially painted for him. I was shown a photo of it by a woman who had visited the Jung home. It was the STAR+GATE pattern almost line for line. Where it differed, ever so slightly, it expressed inner aspects of the Circle Pattern that only I knew about.

○ In 1981, I met a woman named Susan through a friend. She took one look at the Circle Pattern and said, "Oh, that's just like Arthur Young's theory of consciousness." She went on to explain how this man's theory, which had been developed over the last twenty years, corresponded to the different levels and divisions within the pattern. A few weeks later she invited me to show STAR+GATE to a group that studied personal growth. After showing them the game, a young artist took me aside. She wanted to show me her sketchbook. She explained she had been doing studies of circles and dimensions. She flipped through page after page of various drawings of circles and spheres, all done in different, experimental styles. Then she turned to the only sketch that was geometric, and there it was, the Circle Pattern. She had never seen STAR+GATE before, but it was the exact diagram. She was as shocked as I was.

Such parallels and coincidences have occurred increasingly over the years. This is all the more reason why the *Close Encounters* story of a subconscious message moved me so deeply. Whether the movie is seen as a metaphor or taken literally, it seems that something is emerging from within us and that STAR+GATE is a part of it.

STAR+GATE's future role, whatever it may be, will most likely be based on what it already offers us. It is a map and a language—both of which are new to us. The map, the Circle Pattern, the language, the Symbolic Cards—taken together they create an organized approach to dealing with the relatively uncharted area of human thoughts and emotions. As the system is used and explored by more people, it may well become a standard for understanding the interplay in life between the physical and nonphysical, between consciousness and matter, spirit and form.

Since the Symbolic Cards are simple, everyday symbols, the system is accessible to many. There is nothing esoteric or technical that makes it difficult to learn or use. The meaning of the symbols is left up to the player. This fact not only makes it effective for self-exploration, it also opens up possibilities for its use as a language between people for understanding others and for communicating meaning. Like Hesse's bead game, the Circle Pattern and cards can be used to express the intangibles of living between two or more people. It is even possible that the symbols could have new meanings assigned to them, musical notes, for example, so musicians could communicate in their own discipline. The potential could be broadened by adding correspondences from other disciplines. The use of the Circle Pattern along with the cards themselves could also indicate relationships within a discipline that would have additional meaning for the players.

All this merely hints at the possibilities ahead. You yourself may glimpse potentials as you read this. It is all part of a dream that is gradually coming to life. We are each both a part of the dream and the one who dreams it. I trust to you and to life that we will unfold it beautifully, discovering in the end the rich meaning of it all.

APPENDIX

● ▲ ✦ ▼ ✕ ◖ ■

THE GOAL SPREAD

The Goal Spread is a relatively quick and easy three-card array. It provides a way to visualize specific goals and portray the blocks to those goals, and it leads to a plan for getting the desired results.

The spread was originally designed for people who did not like drawing cards randomly from the deck. Therefore, it calls for choosing the cards to be used. It is also such a simple spread that no spread sheet is required.

Here are the instructions for the Goal Spread:

1. With a specific topic or situation in mind, choose one of the Symbolic Cards from the deck to symbolize your goal, what you want to see happen. Make your selection based on the picture side of the card alone. Place the "Goal" card out in front of you.

2. Next choose a card that symbolizes what is keeping you from getting the goal. What is the problem, what blocks you from having what you want? Once this card is chosen, place it in front of you just below the "Goal" card.

3. Choose a third card that symbolizes yourself in the particular situation, something that describes where you are in terms of the "Goal" and "Problem" cards. Once chosen, place this card below the other two in front of you.

4. Begin interpreting the cards by turning all three over to the word side. Discover what Card Types are in each position in the spread and see what this reveals about the idea of "Goal," "Problem," and "You" in terms of your topic. Also, read the words associated with each symbol and see how they relate to the positions within the spread.

5. Next, make Picture Stories with pairs of cards in the following manner. Place the "Goal" card with the "You" card and make a mental picture with these two. Once you can describe what the picture looks like, discover what it is telling you about yourself and your goal. Then place the "You" card with the "Problem." Make a mental picture with these two and see what it is telling you about yourself and the blocks to success. Then put the "Problem" and "Goal" cards together in a mental picture; see what it says about how the problem interacts with the desired result. Finally, make a Picture Story with all three cards together, and discover how they interact when all elements are present. This can be a very telling picture.

THE GOAL SPREAD

GOAL

PROBLEM

YOU

6. Now create a Best Picture with the three symbols. Visualize the very best looking picture you can that includes all three elements. Discover what the picture means in terms of your situation. What kinds of action or what new approach does it indicate? This is a symbolic plan of action for dealing with the block and getting to the goal you want.

Interpreting this spread is based on the Six-Step Process discussed on pages 7–9. You may wish to refer to that section for more detailed information on the Picture Story portion of the process. Also, some people may prefer to draw their cards from the deck rather than choose them, which is quite acceptable.

RELATIONSHIP SPREAD

Here is a spread that two people can use at once. Many people use STAR+GATE to explore relationships of one kind or another, whether it be a love relationship, a family or a business relationship, or any other way one can be a partner. The Sky Spread is adequate for such topics, but it shows a picture that is based only on the player's *own* perspective. To allow two partners to play at once and for both to have their own perspectives revealed, the following alterations are provided.

1. The Sky Spread arrangement is used, but the boxes are renamed for the A partner, the B partner, and the two together as shown.

2. The person chosen to be A shuffles and cuts the deck of cards. The A person then draws the first card and places it in box A1; the next card drawn goes into A2; the third into A3.

3. The person chosen as B then shuffles the deck, cuts, and draws three cards, placing them in B1, B2, and B3.

4. Together, A and B shuffle, cut, and draw the cards for boxes AB1 to AB4. Share the procedure of shuffling and drawing in any way desired.

5. Together, A and B interpret their cards using the Six-Step Process of Interpretation (see pages 7–9).

OUR ISSUE

A'S ISSUE

B'S ISSUE

AB4

A3

B3

A1   A2   AB1   B1   B2

US NOW

A NOW   B NOW

DISTRACTING US   AB3   AB2   HELPING US

6. Boxes A1 and A2 refer to A's own present, with A's Issue above as a personal focus of attention. B's own boxes are the same for B. For the AB boxes, "Us Now" describes the two as a couple or as partners, with "Our Issue" being the current issue they are facing together or their common focus of attention. The "Helping" and "Distracting" symbols can belong to either or both; it is up to the players to decide.

The complete Six-Step Process is recommended because of what the Picture Story part can reveal, of the sharing required to perform it, and because of the value to both people in creating a Best Picture together. This can result in an enhanced approach on the part of both partners that will greatly benefit the relationship.

USING **STAR+GATE** WITH CHILDREN

Children respond readily to the visual images in STAR+ GATE, and you may be pleasantly surprised at how much value they can receive from playing with the system in various ways.

THE "STORYBOOK" GAME

Especially creative (and many times revealing) is an activity called Storybook. This is a cooperative game in which players build a story using images from the cards. From a shuffled deck of cards, the first player draws a card and begins a story using the image on that card. For instance, if the Rope card is drawn, the first player might say, "Once there was a rope lying on the ground." Then the next player draws a card and adds to the story. If the next card is the Magician, that player might say, "Once there was a rope lying on the ground, and along came a magician who made it rise into the air." The play continues until twelve cards have been drawn. Then each player has the opportunity to create the best ending for the story.

This is an excellent game to play with children, and they can play it on their own at this level. An alternate version of this, good as an icebreaker among adults, is to deal each player a hand of five cards and let them choose which card to play in a continuing story.

SKY SPREAD USE

Children from about the age of nine or ten can use STAR+GATE with the Sky Spread or other spreads with the introduction and guidance of someone older or experienced with STAR+GATE. Even though not all the words on the cards will be understood, the visual symbols allow ample means for young people to develop meanings and express their thoughts about particular subjects of interest.

In addition, family members can use STAR+GATE together, exploring relationships between individuals or focusing on a specific topic.

LIST OF SYMBOLIC CARDS

STARS (A–L)

A. Star of Impulse (page 48)
B. Star of Reaching (page 49)
C. Star of Change (page 50)
D. Star of Inwardness (page 51)
E. Star of Laugh (page 52)
F. Star of Bowing (page 53)
G. Star of Indecision (page 54)
H. Star of Hope (page 55)
I. Star of Austerity (page 56)
J. Star of Independence (page 57)
K. Star of Aspiration (page 58)
L. Star of Patience (page 59)

STATES (1–12)

1. Sand (page 62)
2. Lightning (page 63)
3. Rain (page 64)
4. Mud (page 65)
5. Fire (page 66)
6. Water (page 67)
7. Earth (page 68)
8. Thunder (page 69)
9. Snow (page 70)
10. Fog (page 71)
11. Air (page 72)
12. Pool (page 73)

STAR-CROSSES (13–36)

13. Magician (page 76)
14. Lover (page 77)
15. Child (page 78)
16. Egg (page 79)
17. Moon (page 80)
18. Jester (page 81)
19. Maiden (page 82)
20. Butterfly (page 83)
21. Knight (page 84)
22. Swan (page 85)
23. Sun (page 86)
24. Monk (page 87)
25. Wanderer (page 88)
26. Tree (page 89)
27. Chest (page 90)
28. Glass (page 91)
29. Duck (page 92)
30. Leaf (page 93)
31. Bell (page 94)
32. Knife (page 95)
33. Ladder (page 96)
34. Window (page 97)
35. Fountain (page 98)
36. Candle (page 99)

GLOSSARY

● ▲ ✚ ▼ ✖ ◗ ■

Many common words are used in the STAR+GATE system in new ways. These special designations are explained in the following glossary.

Card Types   Groupings of STAR+GATE's ninety-six Symbolic Cards into seven categories, each descriptive of a level of personal experience.

Circle Pattern   The circular, mandalalike geometric design that is the visual core of the STAR+GATE system.

Circuits   A technique for examining connections between STAR+GATE cards once the symbols' positions have been plotted on the Circle Pattern.

Cycle of Growth   The series of Houses and Seas within the STAR+GATE Circle Pattern that describes the classic stages of progress of the individual. This is related to the mythology of the zodiac, to the Houses and Signs in astrology, and to other models of human psychology.

Garden   The distinctly interior section within a House area on the Circle Pattern.

Gates   One of the seven STAR+GATE Card Types. Gates represent attitudes and approaches of the individual.

Gifts   A Card Type designation that describes an individual's inner talents and abilities.

Goal Spread   A three-card layout for the STAR+GATE cards. It is designed to focus on achieving a desired result.

Houses   The twelve basic divisions of the STAR+GATE Circle Pattern used to describe a classic Cycle of Growth. Each House contains a group of STAR+GATE symbols.

Keys   One of the seven Card Types. They represent various challenges that can lead to personal realizations.

Level of Approach   The term used with the "You Now" symbol in a spread of STAR+GATE cards to emphasize the individual's current position as one of seven possible levels.

Picture Stories The technique used in interpreting STAR+ GATE Cards. It entails imagining the interaction of groups of symbols to reveal subconscious knowledge about personal topics.

Relationship Spread The Sky Spread format with card positions renamed in order to display aspects of personal relationships.

Seas The twelve areas on the Circle Pattern that supplement the series of twelve Houses. These contain groups of STAR+GATE symbols and, as a series, they restate the Cycle of Growth described by the Houses.

Signs One of the seven STAR+GATE Card Types. They represent aspects of personal fulfillment or satisfaction.

Sky Spread The spread or layout for STAR+GATE cards. It includes present, past, and future aspects of a personal topic.

Star-crosses One of the seven Card Types. These cards stand for kinds of self-expressions, "sides" of oneself that are shown to others.

Stars One of the seven Types of STAR+GATE Cards. Stars represent fundamental energies involved in situations and in individuals. The Stars are component energies that comprise or "build" all other STAR+GATE symbols, as seen by their interaction on the Circle Pattern.

States The Card Type designation that represents outer conditions and kinds of circumstances involved in personal situations.

Storybook A story-telling and memorization game for children using the STAR+GATE symbols.

Synchronicity A term first used by psychologist Carl Jung to describe the connectedness and appropriateness of seemingly unrelated events experienced in life.

FOR FURTHER INFORMATION

If you'd like more information on STAR+GATE accessories and educational activities write to:

STAR+GATE Enterprises
P.O. Box 1006
Orinda, CA 94563